W9-APT-316

josh@josh

josh@joshdavis.com

josh@joshdavis.com

John Ashley Null

Real Joy

Freedom to be Your Best

Real Joy

Freedom to be Your Best

Bestell-Nr. 393.966

ISBN 3-7751-3966-4

PRINTING AND BINDING:
Ebner & Spiegel, Ulm (Printed in Germany)

EXCLUSIVE RIGHT FOR DISTRIBUTION BY
Hänssler Verlag, D-71087 Holzgerlingen
and SRS PRO SPORTLER e.V., D-57610 Altenkirchen

DESIGN
LATSCH DESIGN, D-57548 Kirchen

PHOTO CREDITS
Bongarts Sportphoto, MEV, Photodisc, SRS PRO SPORTLER

To Jay, Josh, JJ, and Ben

They shared with me their world of sports,
In hopes that
I would share with them what I knew of God.

CONTENTS

FOREWORD
JOSH DAVIS

Olympic Village, Sydney, Australia, 2000

Dear Fellow Athlete,

> But by the grace of God
> I am what I am,
> and his grace to me
> was not without effect.
> No, I worked harder
> than all of them
> – yet not I,
> but the grace of God
> that was with me.
>
> 1 Corinthians 15:10

Some folks today think that spiritual matters are as compatible with sports as fire is with ice. Put fire and ice together, and they will destroy each other – the fire will turn the ice into water, and the water will then put out the fire. Put God and sports together, according to many coaches, and religious faith will destroy an athlete's competitive drive. Put God and sports together, according to many ministers, and athletic success will only teach the believer to think he is important instead of God. The truth is, God and sports not only can go together, they need to go together. Only developing the spirit and the body together can bring out the best in each. Athletes must have spiritual strength to hold on to their athletic dreams through all the hard times they must endure to be one day the best, the very best. And the discipline and focus learned in sport can be of invaluable help in following

God. The Spirit and sports each fire a passion for the other. I should know. I'm a Christian, and I won three gold medals in swimming at the 1996 Olympic Games (the 4x100m medley relay, the 4x100m free relay and the 4x200m free relay).

This evening I had the privilege of representing my country once again here in Sydney. The race was the biggest in my life – the fastest ever Olympic final of my favorite event, the 200m freestyle! Fourteen years of training culminated in just 1 minute and 46 seconds! You can imagine the intensity of emotion as so many thoughts ran through my mind. I asked God for His grace, wisdom and strength. Purposefully, I gave my doubts, fear, and worries to Him, and renewed my mind with God's truth and remembered the lessons I learned from reading my good friend's book, *Real Joy*. Allow me to tell you what happened in my Olympic race and how reading this book over the years has helped me to enjoy and make the most of every situation.

As the eight finalists gathered in the Ready Room, we knew it would be a four-man race: Ian the Aussie favorite, Peter the flying Dutchman, Massi the fast Italian and me, the lone American. Four of the best swimmers in the world but there were only three medals to be had. We looked at each other and knew that one of us would not get a medal.

As we filed into the darkened hallway before marching onto the brightly lit pool deck, all I could see were the huge shoulders of Ian in front of me. At 6′ 5″, 220 lbs, unbeaten in years, he was an intimidating opponent. The two-minute wait to march out seemed more like two hours. I quickly prayed against thoughts of fear, resting in God's provision. Like so many times before, I knew He would give me what I needed when I needed it, and not a second too soon. Next the inescapable moment: the monotone voice echoed throughout the venue, "Please welcome the finalists in the men's 200m freestyle." As we walked out from under the awning, a wave of lights and noise from the 18,000 cheering fans greeted us. The deafening crowd had been anticipating this race for days, and I couldn't help but smile and embrace that amazing moment.

Right before the race the official called us to the blocks, and I said one last prayer: "Lord, help me to go all out for You and with You, regardless of time or place. Thank you for being with me. Let's have some fun!" In just a few seconds the amazingly loud crowd came to a complete silence. "Swimmers take your mark." The thought went through my mind that thirty thousand miles in training over the last 14 years were now coming down to one moment in time.

Bang! The starter's gun released me into the water to race just 200 meters. I felt great and touched ahead in world record pace on the 1st turn at the 50m mark. By halfway at the 100m turn, Peter, Ian and I were right together, and Massi the Italian was a whole meter behind us. On the last turn at the 150m mark Peter and Ian were tied for first, I was right behind them, and the Italian was still a meter behind me. With one length to go, I was in a solid third, and if I held that spot I could win the Bronze medal! All of a sudden the Italian caught up to me, and he and I were neck and neck, stroke for stroke, and in the final meters we put our heads down and reached for the wall. I looked up at the score board and saw the number 4 next to my name. The Dutchman had won, with the Aussie second, and the Italian had touched me out for third place. My heart sunk.

They say that 4th place is the worst place in the Olympics to be in because, whether you're last place or 4th place, neither of you receives a medal. But I looked at my time, and I saw that I had swam a 1:46.7! It broke my own American record by a good margin and would have easily won the previous Olympics. I realized that my prayer had been answered! God was with me during the race, so that I could swim my best, and He was with me now! God had been glorified, and I had swam faster than ever before. I was part of the greatest 200m freestyle race of all time.

Even though I was pleased with my time, after an Olympic final there is a tremendous release of emotion. I was overwhelmed with disappointment for missing a medal by seven one-hundredths of a second. I trained so hard for so long, and to miss my goal by such a small margin stung bitterly. To be honest, I cried and cried and cried. Although I know it's just a piece of metal, I could not separate my emotions from the reality of having sacrificed so much. But that's the beauty of a genuine relationship with God. We can be totally human, vulnerable, honest, and real. Despite that my feelings didn't line up with God's truth at that moment, I could still trust Him and still had joy. Happiness comes and goes, intense sadness comes and goes, but real joy is always there, regardless of the circumstance. I finally found comfort and strength by remembering the fact that God loves me unconditionally and was proud of me for my dependence on Him and sacrifice to Him.

It can be tough when you come from a country where winning is everything. In our cultural economy, performance determines worth, but in God's economy, Christ's performance determines value. During these Olympics *Real Joy* reminded me that my worth was already established forever by Jesus Christ's death on the cross. No gold medal will make Jesus love me any more that He did by dying for me when I was still rejecting him. And a silver medal, fourth place or even last place certainly didn't mean that God is not for me either. Tonight I fully enjoyed the thrill of racing, because Jesus' unconditional, unwavering love for me has freed me from any lingering doubts about my own worth, even when I wasn't no. 1.

I'm reminded that God is not really for me to win the gold, and beat this person, or even break that record. And God is certainly not against me. God wants me to set myself apart, giving my all, acknowledging His presence and relying on His power and His peace. I know that my purpose in life and in swimming is to race all-out regardless of place, to God's glory. But how did I learn to apply these truths? Practically what does that look like? *Real Joy* is a great tool to help make it possible.

I'm excited that you have chosen to supplement your Bible reading with *Real Joy*. This handbook contains biblical principles and promises that were vital to my preparation as a college athlete, professional athlete, Olympian and even as a husband and father.

I recommend that you take your time and read it slowly and meditatively. And it's just the right size to be read again and again. I take it with me on my national team trips, and it's a good resource for chapel ideas and group discussions.

It's always good to be reminded of several things:
1) the purpose of my life and gifts.
2) Christianity is not a crutch or an excuse but the truth, and applicable and relevant to every area of life, even sports.
3) God, our Heavenly Daddy, loves you and me with the most wonderful, special and permanent love!

I know this handbook will help, whether you're dead last or on the top podium as a champion. I've been at both, and having

Real Joy helped me keep perspective and get ever closer to my potential. I wish you God's best for your career and relationships.

Because of His Grace,
Josh Davis

THE ROAD TO BURNOUT

CHAPTER 1

In the heavens [God]
has pitched
a tent for the sun,
which is like
a bridegroom
coming forth
from his pavilion,
like a champion
rejoicing to run
his course.

Psalm 19:4b-5

Sport is supposed to be all about joy. Even the Bible knows that. Psalm 19 parallels the feeling champions get when they do their sport to being on a honeymoon – intense physical satisfaction and emotional contentment all at the same time. You can't get much higher praise for the joy of sport. Every race, every game, every performance is an opportunity to experience afresh the buzz that comes from doing something you really love.

The Joys of Sport

People love sport because they get so much out of it. At its most basic, athletes do sport because it feels good to push yourself physically. When you work your body hard enough, it releases chemicals that counteract the pain, giving you a natural high in the middle of all the strain. But the joy of sport is more than just that it makes your body feel good. Sport can also help you feel good about yourself. Being in top physical condition can give you a body to be proud of. And nothing helps your self-respect like having something in your life which everybody knows you do well. Athletes love sport because it feels good to be good at it.

But the joy doesn't stop there. Sport is a great safety valve. When you're really wound up about something, doing sport is a good way to let off steam. It can also be a great escape hatch from the pressures of every day life. When you're playing sport, you don't have to worry about all the things that get you down when you think about them. So when life gets too much, sport gives athletes a good excuse to spend hours a day forgetting about all their problems and concentrating on something they enjoy doing. In fact, when other things in your life are falling to pieces, sport can easily seem like the one solid thing you can

How do you feel when you exercise? How do you feel when you win?

hold on to. When you feel like that, sport is not merely a way to escape from pressure. It's your reason for living, the purpose in your life that keeps you going. And who doesn't love what makes them feel good about living?

Best of all, however, sport is a ready-made way to find friends. It's really great to be with other people who get just as excited about something as you do. Other athletes like to talk about what you like to talk about. They know just as much about your sporting heroes and their competitors as you do. Other athletes like to do what you like to do. They love to spend as much time practicing their sporting skills as you do. What better basis for friendship can you find? Relationships come easy when you have something as powerful as sport to hold you together. And with sport friendships, much of the time you don't even have to say anything. Each of you knows how much you all get out of being together, going with the flow of the game, instinctively interacting with each other, just sharing the joy of sport. It's only natural to love something that gives you such close friendships.

> Do you relieve stress through sport? If you couldn't do your sport, how would it affect you?

> How many of your friends are in your sport? Do you have any friends outside sport?

Yes, sport is special. It makes your body feel good. It makes you feel good about yourself. It makes you feel good about your life. It even gives you friends it feels good to be with. Very few things in life can claim to offer as much joy as sport does. For many people, sport becomes such an important part of who they are that they want to continue to be active in it long after their best competitive days are over. Although they naturally still like to win if they can, life-long athletes get even more satisfaction from the numerous benefits that come from just continuing to participate. They still enjoy pushing their bodies, even if they cannot push themselves as hard as they used to. It still makes them feel good about themselves to be good at sport, even if they are not as good as they once were. When they need to feel good about their lives, taking time for sport still lets them get away from their every day hassles by concentrating on doing something they really enjoy. And no matter how many times they move or others move on from them, sport still provides a common interest to keep up with old friends and make new ones. While their physical abilities may have faded, their joy from sport has not. The secret to being a life-long sport enthusiast is never losing sight of these joys.

> What motivates you about sport? Is winning more fun than just competing?

That isn't as easy as it sounds, however. America is a very competitive society. So it's hard not to find yourself getting more joy from winning than from just participating. This is especially the case for promising young athletes. Emerging champions burn with a competitive desire to be the best, the very best they can be. Without this fierce passion, they will not have the motivation needed to make the incredible sacrifices that are required to reach the top. It is this fire in their belly that fuels their determination to push their bodies to where few, if anyone, have gone before. If the fire falters, so will their self-discipline. But if the fire gets too intense, they can just as easily burn themselves up, from the inside out. The history of sport is filled with promising young talent who burned out long before they reached their

> Do you know anyone who is burned out on sport?

full potential. And those athletes who keep going with only ashes on the inside often fill the void with an out-of-control, destructive lifestyle. Sadly, the news is full of famous athletes who let their inner fire on the field become a burning rage which batters their loved ones off the field.[1]

When you put your heart and soul into sport, you don't expect it to lead to total burnout. How can something even the Bible says is so good end up causing heartache and harm? Well, it doesn't happen all at once. It's a slow process. And it doesn't happen to everyone, not even to all top athletes. Still, many people get less out their sporting life than they had originally hoped for. And the purpose of this book is to help you avoid that kind of disappointment. So there's no better place to start than by tracing the slow process of how a sporting career can all go wrong. And just as there's no better way to learn how to play sport than by looking at top athletes, there's no better way to see how you can lose your joy than by looking at what can happen to top athletes who are supposed to have it all.

The Loss of Joy

People get their first taste of the joys of sport as children. It doesn't take kids long to discover that play is an opportunity to relax and unwind. When you're in a game, you don't have to think about your unfinished homework or the household chores still left to do. Children also soon figure out that playing games is a great way to bond to other people. Is Dad always too busy to stop and talk for very long? Ask him to play catch and look at how quickly he responds. Are you a new kid on the block looking to make friends? Just show your stuff in a neighborhood game and the next time they play, they will come knocking on your door asking you to join them. Finally, children enjoy sport because it gives them a chance to make a name for themselves. It doesn't take long for kids to decide

who's the best athlete. "Let Sally do it, she's the fastest." "With that arm Marc has got to be our quarterback." And one of the privileges of being a child is that you can spend hours dreaming of how big you're going to make it in sport when you grow up. You replay over and over again in your mind that great day when you will beat your sport hero in a match never to be forgotten by anyone.

As a child, were you picked first, in the middle, or last for the team?

Release, relationships, and a reputation, these are the three childhood joys of sport. As children grow older, however, young people who truly excel at sport begin to enjoy the special recognition that only very good athletes get in America. And the rewards of a great athletic reputation can easily, slowly begin to squeeze out relaxation and relationships. This is how it happens.

The Loss of Release

It doesn't take students long to figure out just how much their success in sport can impress their peers, get the attention of the members of the opposite sex, make their parents proud and even earn them the respect of other adults. And once you have tasted the benefits of winning, outstanding young sportspeople also soon learn that you get to enjoy your privileged status only as long as you stay a winner. You quickly realize that an athlete is as special as his or her current performance. Sport may give you an impressive identity, but you are forced to put that identity on the line every time you step up to the starting line. A bad performance at an important event can easily turn a hero into a has-been in the eyes of the crowd. And when that happens, the crowd will abandon the has-been and move on to the new hero. Once you come to depend on sport to make you feel special, it stops being an escape from pressure.

> Have you felt the joy of being a winner? Have you felt the rejection of being a loser?

Instead, sport becomes the very focus of that pressure. As a result, sport ceases to be about play and becomes all about performance. Sport ceases to be a source of wonder and becomes a steady stream of work.

The Loss of Relationships

To cope with this new pressure, high school champions often feel forced to narrow their focus to just themselves. Friendships become suspect. If you have lost a lot of "friends" during a rough patch in your sporting career, you will be more cautious when the crowd wants to come back now that you are winning again. Even those sports stars who have never suffered through revolving-door friendships can experience the feeling of being used to advance someone else's status. Outstanding athletes are important, and knowing something about an important person that no one else does can make people in the know look important, when they share their inside knowledge with the crowd: "What does Marc think of Joe's ability? He thinks it's garbage. I know because he told me;" or, "Sally says she likes you, but she told me the truth. She really likes Marc and is using you to make

> Do you like your friends because they're good at sport? How do you treat people who are not good? Are you different to people who are really good?

him feel jealous." Once betrayed by those you thought were your friends, it's easy to start wondering, "Do these people really care about me, or are they just interested in what being my friend will do for their reputation?" Experience teaches the high school champion to keep the crowd at arm's length.

Too often you also learn that you must do the same even with fellow athletes. Real friends are people with whom you feel free to be just yourself, whether you're on top of the world celebrating today's victory or scraping the bottom because you are really worried that you might not win the upcoming game. Outstanding teenage athletes are expected by the coach and their teammates to be leaders who set the example. It's your job to show the others how to be mentally tough. It's your job to go around and boost everyone else's confidence. How then can you tell your teammates about your own doubts and fears?

And then there's the envy factor. Teammates can also be competitors, whether for the same position on the squad of a team sport like volleyball or in the same event of an individual sport like swimming. It's hard for those who compete against you to be happy for your success. Even those who don't directly compete against a sports star may feel cheated by the other's success. They may be well-respected by everybody as good high-school athletes. Still, it's difficult for them not to be jealous of someone who seems headed for a big-time college program or even the Olympics. After all, it's the young sports star who's going to get to live the life they have always dreamed about. It's especially hard not to be envious when an average high school athlete trains just as hard as the champion does, if not harder, but the star gets all the recognition. Should the champion try to confide to less successful athletes the pressures that come with being at the top, they may show little sympathy for the stresses and struggles that come with the success they feel

> **Have you ever felt cheated? Have you ever been jealous of someone else's success?**

denied. High school sports stars choose to hang out with their fellow athletes rather than with the crowd, but they know that they must still keep up their guard. For them, sport gradually ceases to be about being with friends and becomes more and more just about being out in front of the pack, all by themselves, with few, if any, close friends.

So as young sports stars grow older, their reputation as a winner gradually becomes the only joy sport still offers them. At first, the rewards of winning seem worth the cost. Adolescence is all about peer acceptance, and there is no more certain way to gain the approval and admiration of other Americans than by being a star athlete. Eventually, however, even the joy that comes from being a star begins to fade.

Since being special in sport is the only thing such athletes have going for them, winning becomes the focus of their life. If they don't perform well, they punish themselves emotionally. They tell themselves how no good they are for letting themselves "mess-up" and become a loser. They learn to rely on this self-hatred to force themselves to train harder and longer until they become a winner again.

Unfortunately, even winning is not much better for their emotional health. The thrill of victory is intense, but short-lived. To keep feeling that joy, sports stars must win over and over again. But the more you win, the less joy you get from winning. Like an addict who needs ever higher doses of his drug to enjoy the same high, it is not enough to just win at the same level as before. Having "been there, done that, got the T-shirt," there isn't much emotional kick left in such victories. They become routine, an accomplishment which the champion expects as his or hers

> Do you feel that winning is the "only thing"? Are you out of balance in life in order to become a success in sport?

by right, but providing no thrill. Every victory only increases the need to win the next time at a higher level against more difficult competition for the joy to feel as good as it did before.

It is not surprising, then, that many sport stars begin to feel trapped. A cartoon in the *New Yorker* magazine sums up their situation. Dressed for tennis, holding his dark sunglasses and leaning against his turbo Porsche, a man quips to his friends, "I despise my life, but I'm in love with my life style."[2] They may hate the increasing emptiness of their life as an athlete, but they have become addicted to its lifestyle of perks and privileges. They continue to strain to go forward toward greater sporting success, but only because they refuse to go back to being just another face in the crowd.

To ensure more and better victories as they grow older, young sport stars focus all their thoughts on what they must do to win again. Training schedules become a higher priority than being with other people. And since their thoughts are dominated by what they need to do to be a winner, their

Do you think about others or yourself more often? Do you think more about training and winning than about family and friends?

self-preoccupation naturally slips into their conversations when they do spend time with others. The more self-centered they become, the more difficulty they have in making healthy relationships. The more lonely they feel, the more they need to win to keep being a hero in the eyes of the crowd. Having invested all their physical and emotional energy in being a winner, they have ignited within themselves that burning desire necessary for making the sacrifices required to excel to an elite level. Yet, unless they can find something more in life than winning, their inner fire will burn them up from the inside out.

The Road to Burnout

Young champions need relaxation and friendships like anybody else. But when sport no longer meets these needs, it's hard for them to find them somewhere else. Because of the total commitment needed to be on top, growing sports stars don't have much time left over for getting involved in other activities which might help. It shouldn't be surprising, then, that outstanding young athletes often come to rely on three easy crutches for release and relationships – drinking, dating, and sex.

Drinking and Drugs. Sport may no longer provide them with a physical release from day-to-day pressures and a ready-made set of friends. But young champions soon learn that drinking can offer easy access to both. Alcohol, after all, loosens you up. And that can really help you relax and socialize. No problem seems quite so bad at that moment when you're feeling the buzz that comes from drinking. Besides, alcohol lowers your inhibitions so you feel free to "let it all hang out." Feeling frustrated about a personal problem? Drinking will give you the freedom to get aggressive without having to worry about the consequences right away. Feeling depressed? Alcohol can give you the courage to tell even complete strangers your deepest, darkest secrets. Feeling lonely? Drinking can make you feel like you fit in with the people around you who are also drinking. It can even give you the self-confidence you need to get to know someone you find attractive. As sport used to be, drinking can be an activity that helps you unwind and feel part of the group at the same time. Because of these benefits, young champions often make drinking the fireplace for their inner fire.

Do you think the gifted athletes who party hard can continue having success in sport?

Unfortunately, drinking is only a makeshift measure. At first, alcohol and sport can seem to be the perfect combination. Partying off the field eases every day pressures so that athletes can perform when they have to on the field. Performing well on the field gives them the status they need to be able to party off the field. But the more young sports stars excel, the more they feel the pressure to achieve even more. And if they rely on drinking to help them cope, they can easily slide into a downward spiral.

Just imagine what that's like. The pressure on you to do well causes you to seek relief through drinking. But your drinking often leads to destructive behavior which causes you even more problems. The more you mess up in your personal life, the more you cling to sport as the one positive thing you have going. The more you rely on sport to feel good about yourself, the more pressure you feel to be good at it. The more pressure you feel, the more you look to drinking to release it. But there comes a point when your partying off the field begins to undermine your performance on the field, causing you to feel even more pressure. So you rely even more on drinking, which makes it even harder to perform as well as you want to. Once young champions find themselves caught in this downward spiral, it's not surprising that they may try drugs to get an even bigger relief from all the problems that their drinking has caused them. And, of course, drugs only speed up their descent into self-destruction.

> Do you think alcohol and drugs undermine your sports performance and ultimately your potential?

Dating Relationships. Drinking may help you relax and relate to others, but it doesn't give you any real sense of intimacy. For that, emerging champions naturally turn to a steady relationship with a member of the opposite sex. Having a girlfriend or boyfriend provides young athletes with a trusted companion. Here is someone you can just be yourself with, whether it's a good day or a bad day. And when you need to, here is someone you can confide your problems to without fear of being betrayed. A steady relationship also gives young sports stars a regular opportunity for physical intimacy and the release from pressure it offers. As long as the relationship holds, and their sporting success does too, young sports stars feel pretty good about themselves and the life they lead.

Unfortunately, a steady relationship is also only a makeshift fireplace. All too often, the fire inside the athletes is too hot for their companions. It goes without saying that gifted sportspeople expect their "steadies" to understand that training always comes first. Should an athlete like to be alone a few days before a competition to focus, the "steady" must simply learn to live with that ritual as part of the price of the relationship. And because athletes concentrate so much of their attention on what they must do every day for them to stay a winner, they often have very little mental energy left over to be supportive of their "steadies".

Would you say your dating relationships have been affected by your sport? How?

In fact, they can easily approach a girlfriend-boyfriend relationship the same way they do everything else – by asking how it will help them with their athletic performance. Without even realizing it, their attitude toward the other person can easily be: "I want to find someone who will fill this emptiness in my life because I train better when I'm happy." Foremost in their mind is what they are going to get out of the relationship, not what they will enjoy giving to it. Consequently, a relationship with a champion can be fairly one-sided. For that very reason, often the only kind of people interested in being a sport star's "steady" is someone who wants to use being with the athlete to enhance his or her own reputation.

Do you approach relationships concerned about what's in it for you?

When both people in a relationship focus on what the other person is going to do for them, rather than on what they enjoy doing for that person, the relationship rarely stands the test of time. This is especially true when you're living under the constant pressure of having to prove yourself. Emotions swing back and forth from high highs to low lows with dizzying speed. You can quite easily read rejection into innocent actions, jump to conclusions, and get your feelings hurt. When two self-centered young people have a relationship, every week provides plenty of opportunity for each to feel slighted by the other.

When the quarrels become too intense, too often athletes will want to bail out. After all, the purpose of having a "steady" was to find someone who would make your life better so you could concentrate on training. When the relationship becomes just one more pressure, one more source for emotional pain, it becomes a threat to your ability to focus on your performance. What happens when the steady relationship breaks down? The former companion often tells other people the champion's confidences, making athletes more reluctant to trust a future "steady" quite so much. Emerging sports stars often learn to sacrifice emotional intimacy as the price of continuing to win.

Casual Sex. When star athletes give up on real emotional intimacy, random sexual relations can often become a convenient substitute. After all, "one-night stands" provide more physical release and intimate personal interaction than drinking, and they don't carry with them the demands of a dating relationship! But sexual promiscuity is also only a makeshift fireplace. For using sex as a way to cope with pressure can be just as addictive and destructive as drinking or doing drugs. When stress seriously builds up, the promiscuous athlete may find it hard to resist the thrill of

> Would the peace of mind of knowing you had no guilt, no STDs, no shame, no unwelcome pregnancies help you perform better?

sex as an adventure into unexplored, even hostile, territory. In recent years the news has been full of famous athletes whose compulsion to satisfy their sexual desires has led them

to questionable actions and landed them in court and even prison. Casual sex, like drinking and dating, cannot permanently contain a young sports star's burning desire to be the best, the very best. And the end result is often burnout in a blaze of destructive behavior.

The End of the Line. This downward spiral towards burnout can take years. For many outstanding athletes, it's only after they turn professional that they begin to feel the devastating results of years of living by makeshift measures. The demand for perfection by fans and management can be as enormous as the salaries many professional athletes command. Only constant success can satisfy the expectations of others and their own egos. And the money only makes it easier to fuel destructive ways to relieve some of this increased pressure. Imagine what that's like. Big-league salaries can finance spending sprees to indulge your personal whims or to buy a few friends. With that kind of money you can purchase plenty of cocaine or place big gambling bets, or even beat a wife who you think won't leave you because she knows you're the best meal-

> How many pro athletes do you think live on the road to destruction: 10%? 50%? 70%? 90%?

ticket she will ever have. The longer sports stars continue to drive themselves to be the very best while relying on destructive habits to cope with the consequences, the greater the likelihood that their instability off the field will catch up with them, either through adverse publicity or by undermining their athletic performance. If given enough time, eventually their addiction to the downward spiral will destroy their sporting career and their capacity to have a decent life afterwards. The inner passion of these elite athletes will burn through their makeshift fireplaces, leaving them burned out and those around them burned up.

Summary

Every athlete grows up dreaming of becoming a superstar. Who hasn't spent countless afternoons practicing by pretending over and over again that you are scoring the winning come-from-behind touchdown in the Superbowl or sinking the winning three point swisher as the buzzer sounds in the NCAA finals? As you go through the motions over and over again, each time you feel the sense of pride rising up inside as you score. Each time you can hear the roar of the crowd tell you how special you are because you are a winner. Each time you think of all the people who will want to be your friend when you become a somebody. Even if your level of ability doesn't open you up to the same intensity of pressures as the superstars, your own competitive drive to make your mark can be just as consuming. Without even noticing it, you can begin to focus so much on how great it will be when you win some big sporting goal that you don't take time to enjoy the good things along the journey. Without even noticing it, you can begin to base so much of your self-esteem on how great it is to be a winner that you lose the joy of sport. When you sacrifice everything to win, you will eventually discover that winning isn't enough. That's why so many winners in sport are losers in life. But you don't have to be. There is a better way.

What is your sports dream?

Have you missed out on something in life because of sport? If you could do it all over, what would you do differently?

WHAT MAKES US TICK

Yet, O Lord,
you are our Father.
We are the clay,
you are the potter;
we are all
the work
of your hand.

Isaiah 64:8

The meaning of life can seem a great mystery. That's why it's the perfect topic to spend endless late night hours going around and around debating with friends because no one really seems to know the answer. Not even Lucy from the *Peanuts* cartoon strip really knows. She tells Charlie Brown, "The whole trouble with you is you don't understand the meaning of life." "Do you understand the meaning of life?" he asks her. Lucy replies, "We're not talking about me, we're talking about you!"[3] The secret to having a great life can easily seem to be "out there" somewhere, held by someone else, far off and out of our reach. The truth is that the meaning of life is not found on the top of a steep mountain or in the stars of the Milky Way, but in the depths of our own heart. The key to understanding the meaning and purpose of life is to understand what makes us tick. Only then can we ever hope to know what will really make us feel fulfilled.

Probably one question about life more than any other haunts the minds of champions – "Why am I not satisfied?" Everybody keeps telling superstars how good they have it. Their friends and admirers think that all the perks and privileges that come with being a champion should make them happy. It's not surprising, then, that superior sportspeople are confused when their private lives fail to live up to everybody's expectations, including their own! And it's difficult for them to know where to turn to find an answer to their problem. After all, so many people are looking to them as leaders, role models, and concrete examples of the American dream. If, like Lucy, everybody thinks you have the answer to having a great life, but you know you don't, it's hard to know where to look for help. Who can you turn to?

Why not God? If you don't understand why you're not satisfied, then you don't really understand yourself. And who better to explain to you what makes you tick than the One who made you? That's why God has given us the Bible. When something is not working properly in your car,

Have you ever talked to God or read the Bible? Do you find the Bible is hard to read or is intimidating? Do you think the Bible is relevant to your life?

you turn to the manufacturer's manual which explains how the car was put together. If you want to understand how the human heart was put together, it only makes sense to look at the information provided by our Maker in his "manufacturer's guide," the Bible.

Human Nature: God's Design

Then God said, "Let us make man in our image, in our likeness, and let them rule over the fish of the sea and the birds of the air, over the livestock, over all the earth, and over all the creatures that move along the ground." (Genesis 1:26)

According to the Bible, human beings were made in God's image. That means, like God, we have the capacity to think, to create, and to achieve. That's why sportspeople can dream of doing great deeds, set long-term goals toward achieving them, and use their will-power to make the necessary daily sacrifices along the way. But above all else, God is Love. Because we are made in his image, God has also designed human beings to be creatures who need more than anything else to give and to receive love. No matter how many achievements you have, only knowing that you are really loved can make you feel fully alive. As any champion can tell you, no athletic victory seems complete until you have pushed past the congratulating crowds, found your family and friends, and shared your joy with them.

Have you ever won something in sport and your family wasn't there? Does it make a difference when they are there?

No matter how great our success, we still find our deepest

fulfillment in loving relationships. That's why God made families. By divine plan, life-long love and human life are supposed to be inseparable. Human life should begin from the love of a man and a woman who are committed to spending their lives together. When their love produces children, they are supposed to grow up in a home filled with that life-long love. When their children become old enough to give to someone else the life-long love they have received from their parents, they are to find a partner, marry, and in time start a loving family of their own. Life-long love gives birth to life, life gets its joy from life-long love – that's the God-designed cycle which is at the root of human nature.

Do you hope to marry and have a family some day?

But why does being loved for a lifetime bring us such joy? Think about your old mitt or your favorite pair of running shoes. No matter how worn down they have become, you still love them because of all the good times you have had with them. Suppose they could talk back and tell you what it felt like to have you care about them so much. Margery Williams imagines just that in her book about children's toys.

> *For a long time the Velveteen Rabbit lived on the nursery floor. Being only made of velveteen, some of the expensive mechanical toys quite snubbed him and pretended they were real. They made the poor little Rabbit feel very insignificant and commonplace, and the only toy who was kind to him at all was the Skin Horse. The Skin Horse had lived longer in the nursery than any of the others, and he was wise. "What is REAL?" asked the Rabbit one day. "Does it mean having things that buzz inside you and a stick-out handle?" "Real isn't how you are made," said*

the Skin Horse. "It's a thing that happens to you. When a child loves you for a long, long time, not just to play with, but REALLY loves you, then you become Real." "Does it happen all at once, like being wound up," he asked, "or bit by bit?" "It doesn't happen all at once," said the Skin Horse. "You become. It takes a long time. Generally, by the time you are Real, most of your hair has been loved off, and your eyes drop out and you get loose in the joints and very shabby. But these things don't matter at all, because once you are Real you can't be ugly, except to people who don't understand. Once you are Real, you can't become unreal again. It lasts for always."[4]

What makes human beings REAL? It's not keeping yourself busy buzzing around. Doing lots of activities can help you develop your talent, but if you spend all your time running around you can easily end up becoming a mechanical soldier pretending to have a life. Nor is it having lots of fancy handles by which people instantly recognize you. No matter how thrilling it is to hang a World Series pennant in your living room or wear a couple of Super Bowl rings on your hand, they are only testimonies to your talent as an athlete. And all athletic talent fades with age. When the crowds shift their attention to younger players, former champions can easily end up feeling like a piece of worn-out old sports equipment abandoned in favor of a newer model.

> Do you feel special because of your sports achievements?

Being REAL only happens when you know that you're valued not for what you do, but for who you are as a person. An old well-used mitt can be priceless to its owner. No matter how banged up it has become, the mitt remains forever beautiful in his or her eyes because of all the love that prompted its use. The athlete's lasting love for the mitt gives it a value that does not fade away. All human beings need to be loved with that kind of unconditional, unchanging love. Only really being loved for who we are on the inside can make us feel like we have real lasting value. Life-long love gives joy to life because only that kind of love has the power to make us feel like we have a worth that won't go away.

Not all kinds of love last a lifetime. Erotic love just wants to get sexual gratification with someone else for the moment. Conditional love is willing to give emotional support to someone else, but only if it is assured of getting back as much as it is giving out. It's the kind of 50/50 love that says, "I will love

> Do you want to be loved because of your talent or because of your being a REAL person?

you just as much as you love me, but if I find I'm giving more emotional support to you than you are to me, then I won't love you anymore unless you start giving as much as me." As the Skin Horse described, the love that last a lifetime is an unconditional and unchanging commitment to love someone else no matter what happens. Christians call this kind of very special love by the Greek word for it in the Bible – αγαπη. In English, the word is written as "agape" and pronounced "AG-a-pay".

Have you ever experienced unconditional love? Do you see a need in your life for this kind of love?

The highest form of love, agape gives without expecting to get anything in return. It values other people as they really are, never expecting that they be something they're not. It always continues to love – continuing to love us through the bad times as well as the good, continuing to love us when we're easy to love and when we're not, continuing to love us whether our weight is up or our competitive performance down, continuing to love us even when we've decided

What percentage of pro athletes do you think experience agape love?

for the time being not to love back. Because it's always there, agape love makes people feel valuable deep down, regardless of their current actions and achievements. At its best, through the years the love of families and friends can approach the high standards of agape love. According to the Bible, however, only God loves us from the very beginning with consistent, perfect agape love.

Since God is love, he wants to express that love. He created us in his image so he could lavish his love on us, and we could love him in return. Of all the wonders of creation, the most spectacular is that God Almighty designed human beings for the purpose of having a meaningful relationship with him. The Bible's claim that humanity can know their Maker in a personal way can easily seem to make about as much sense as saying we can shake hands with a star or drink the Milky Way.

But an honest human heart knows better, for God has so fashioned us that our hearts are restless until we rest in his love.

> Apart from God's love do you feel a void, a restlessness?

Apart from God, we are incomplete and inconsistent. No matter how much we are loved by other people, without God's agape love in our lives, our sense of self-worth is like a roller-coaster. It's up and down according to all the chances and changes of life. If things go well, if we win the match, if we get good grades or a nice raise, if that someone special decides we're special, everything is fine . . . for a while . . . until things go poorly. If we get injured or lose the game; if we get poor grades or lose our job; if we're hurt by the one we love; or worse, realize that we've hurt the one we love; or worse yet, realize we have no one to love – life seems rotten. Our moods can swing, our actions can be erratic. And in the end we die, and our bodies rot. Only God's love in our hearts can give us confidence in our self-worth that goes beyond our current circumstances. In fact, only God's love in our hearts can give us

> What else do people use besides God to give them peace, purpose, value?

assurance of eternal life in the face of the certainty of death. God has created human beings to need a life-long relationship with him above all others. For only his agape love gives us a sense of worth and value that lasts forever.

Human Nature Now:
Enslaved to the Enemy's Game Plan

Be self-controlled and alert. Your enemy the devil prowls around like a roaring lion looking for someone to devour.
(I Peter 5:8)

As every top athlete knows, after a certain level, what separates winners from losers is not physical ability but mental toughness. That's why a key part of some athletes' competitive strategy is the "psych." Trash talk, physical intimidation, showing ice-cold nerves under pressure, a "psycho" stare – it's all part of the game to make your opponents doubt their ability to be as good as you. If you can beat your opponents in their mind, you will eventually beat them on the field. Once people begin to doubt what they can do, they don't try as hard to do it. The less they try, the less they are able to do, and that just makes them doubt themselves even more. Having lost the mental edge, their performance gradually gets worse and worse. Eventually, frustrated that they don't seem to be able ever to get it right, they give up trying altogether. The psych has done its job.

> Do you consider yourself to be mentally tough? Do you try to "psyche" others out in your sport? Have you ever given up because you knew you weren't going to win?

In life, as in sport, the mental game is crucial for success. Since no one has a perfect life, whether the glass is half empty or half full all depends on your mental attitude. If you have a positive attitude, you can ride out bad times and keep working toward better ones. If you give in to a

> Would you say that you have a positive or a negative mental attitude?

negative attitude, however, no matter how many good things come your way, it's never enough. Your glass will always seem half empty. In the end, a negative attitude almost always produces a negative result.

Because God wants a loving relationship with you, he designed you to need him in your life to be content. If you have a relationship with God, you can keep a positive mental attitude, regardless of your circumstances, because having his love in your heart makes you feel good about yourself. Yet from the very beginning of humankind, an enemy has been at work in this world to turn humanity away from finding our self-worth in

Do you think you can thrive apart from God?

God's love for us. Today his negative, destructive power seeks to stop you from reaching your full God-given potential by psyching you out of what God wants to give you.

His strategy is amazingly simple but quite effective. He tries to make you doubt that God loves you so that you feel like you have constantly to prove that you have value. The force of destruction constantly whispers that you can only rely on your abilities to make you feel good about who you are. But, of course, no matter how hard you try to prove your self-worth, it is never enough to satisfy that negative, nagging inner voice. No matter how much you use your talents to achieve, it's never enough to make you feel fulfilled. As a result, you always feel that you still have something more you must prove. When you come to accept this treadmill as the nature of life, the pysch has worked.

The Bible tells us in Genesis 3 that this pattern got established way back in the Garden of Eden. The serpent (the force of destruction) saw Adam and Eve (the first two human beings) as competitors. God had placed humanity in charge of caring for his creation. But the serpent was the most crafty animal, and he wanted to be the ruler. So he used his skill to try to better his position at the expense of Adam and Eve. He knew that God had designed human beings to need his love in their hearts to function at their full abilities. If he was going to be able to defeat Adam and Eve, the serpent had to isolate them from God, their source of strength and power. Since he knew God would never abandon them, the serpent's only hope was to turn their minds away from God and get them to rely on themselves instead.

> The serpent knew God would never abandon Adam and Eve. His only hope was to turn their minds away from God so they would rely on themselves instead.

Let's look at how he did it:

Now the serpent was more crafty than any of the wild animals the LORD God had made. He said to the woman, "Did God really say, 'You must not eat from any tree in the garden'?" The woman said to the serpent, "We may eat fruit from the trees in the garden, but God did say, 'You must not eat fruit from the tree that is in the middle of the garden, and you must not touch it, or you will die.'" "You will not surely die," the serpent said to the woman. "For God knows that when you eat of it your eyes will be opened, and you will be like God, knowing good and evil." When the woman saw that the fruit of the tree was good for food and pleasing to the eye, and also desirable for gaining wisdom, she took some and ate of it. She also gave some to her husband, who was with her, and he ate it. Then the eyes of both of them were opened, and they realized they were naked; so they sewed fig leaves together and made coverings for themselves. (Genesis 3:1–7)

In this story, we see the game plan that the force of destruction always uses.

Step 1. He tries to plant a negative attitude in you. His method is to get you to concentrate on what you don't have rather than on what you do. With Eve, the serpent overstated the restriction that God had put on humanity: "Did God really say, 'You must not eat from any tree in the garden'?" Eve set the serpent straight.

> Do you feel entitled to get what you want in life?

It was the fruit of only one tree they could not eat, and only because it would cause them to die. But the serpent had

managed to switch Eve's focus from all the good things God had given her to the one thing he had withheld.

With athletes today, the force of destruction tries to get you to focus on the things you don't like about your life. He may point out the many drawbacks that can come with competitive sport: having to put up with a coach that doesn't understand you, having to live with a training schedule that doesn't let you have any real fun, having to get along with teammates that are a pain, or maybe always failing to achieve a specific victory that you have worked toward for years. Or the force may simply try to get you to fixate on your personal frustrations: having a less-than-ideal family, not having the

> Do you focus on what others have or what you don't have, rather than what you do have?

good things other people have, or maybe not having someone special who really cares for you. Whatever the reason, feeling like you're missing out is the seed of a negative attitude.

Step 2. The force of destruction makes you doubt that God loves you. You don't look for love from someone who mistreats you. So the enemy of humanity tries to make God look unfair in not giving you all that you want. See what the serpent said to Eve. He accused God of denying her the forbidden fruit out of fear of competition: "You will not surely die. For God knows that when you eat of it your eyes will be opened, and you will be like God, knowing good and evil." The serpent wanted Eve to feel cheated so she would decide God really didn't love her after all. The force of destruction uses the same tactic with sportspeople today. Having pointed out all the problems in your life, he says, "If there really was a God who loves you, he would have given you a better deal."

> Do you think God uses hard times to help us grow in maturity?

Step 3. The force undermines your self-esteem for who you are now. Once he has got you to doubt God's love for you, he is able to get you to doubt yourself. How does he do it? He just compares you to others. Naturally, it's effective, because in this life no one has it all. No matter how much talent, ability, and success you have, there is always someone out there who has something you don't. And the force of destruction is always there trying to make you feel inferior by pointing it out. God had made Eve along with Adam ruler over all the creatures he had made. But the serpent made her feel inadequate because she wasn't as wise as God. With athletes today, the enemy is always pointing out the strengths of others and saying, "You aren't smart enough, or athletic enough, or good-looking enough, or rich enough, or popular enough, or witty enough or enough of all those enoughs to feel good enough about yourself to like yourself as you are." Without confidence in God's agape love for you, it's hard not secretly to agree.

Do you feel inadequate? Do you have enough "enoughs"?

Step 4. The force of destruction convinces you to work for your self-worth. With God out of the picture, it's up to you to find a way to feel good enough about yourself. You may not measure up right now, but you can some day, if you use your abilities to make yourself a success. Then, you'll really be somebody special. Then, you'll be just as good, if not even better, than all those people who seem to be better than you right now. That's what the enemy told Eve. God might have been wiser than her at that moment. But if she would use her common sense and eat the fruit, she could become somebody really important. She could become God's equal, not needing to depend on anyone for anything. Then she would never feel inferior again. With sportspeople today, the force of destruction simply says, "Your athletic talent is the ticket to being somebody. When you're number one, then you'll feel good about who you are, then you'll be in control of your life, then people will look up to you as their idol."

How do you make yourself feel important? What are your dreams?

Step 5. The force lies to you that success brings lasting satisfaction. Doubting her own self-worth, but dreaming of how wonderful life was going to be, Eve bit. And so did Adam. And so do so many athletes today. Unsure of themselves unless they're winning, many sportspeople dream of how wonderful it's going to be when they're finally the best, the very best. They pin all their hopes for happiness on being an athletic success. They get through each day hoping that being the champ one day will make up for all they're missing out on today.

But what do they discover in the end? That the force of destruction has pysched them out. Look at Adam and Eve. Doubting God's love for them led them to doubt their own self-worth. But when they tried to "better themselves" without God, they just made things worse. Their disobedience cut them off from God, and they felt naked as a result. Without his agape love in their hearts, they discovered what it was really like to feel inadequate. Yet they had turned their backs on God. All they could do now was turn once again to their own abilities. So they made themselves clothes to try to cover up what was lacking on the inside.

Many athletes today set themselves up for the same kind of disappointment. Stop and think about it. When you look to athletic success to bring you fulfillment,

> What do you expect from your sport? What do you expect from yourself?

you just build up expectations that your achievements can never live up to. Without God's love in your heart, you will always feel like something is missing, no matter how much you succeed. So when you do achieve, disillusionment quickly sets in. You feel a let down which spoils your joy and leaves you feeling more empty on the inside than before you started. But you have committed yourself to finding

> Have you ever felt disillusioned? How do you feel when you're not winning?

happiness through sport. So you simply cover up your current emptiness by setting your sights on a new victory in the future.

Step 6. The enemy's force of destruction makes you his slave. The constant search for satisfaction through accomplishment is futile. That's the whole point behind the hit musical *Little Shop of Horrors*. In the story, a plant with magical powers invades the life of a loser named Seymour.

He brought Seymour more success than he ever dreamed was possible – fame, fortune, and even a beautiful girlfriend. But the plant demanded a price: human blood. And no matter how much blood Seymour provided for the plant, it only grew larger, requiring more blood and singing in a deeper, fuller, more demanding voice, "Feed me, Seymour, feed me!". When we live to satisfy a hunger for achievement, we become a slave to trying to feed it, just as the Bible warns us: "Don't you know that when you offer yourselves to someone to obey him as slaves, you are slaves to the one whom you obey" (Romans 6:16). When you base your self-worth on athletic performance, you become a slave to always having to perform. When you start living by the lies of the force of destruction, you soon find yourself forced to keep following him.

Are you a "slave" to winning or competing in sport?

In a nut shell, here is your life as an athlete. Going along without God's love, you try to satisfy your heart with self-love. You use your abilities to try to find ways to make you like yourself. You set goals such as winning top races or making lots of money. You tell yourself that if you achieve them, you'll be able to feel good about who you are. Soon you can't like yourself unless you are winning. But no matter how much you win, it's never enough to make you feel complete on the inside. Still, winning is the only way you know how to be happy. So as soon as the thrill of victory wears thin, you start looking ahead to the next chance to win again. And the more you succeed, the more you find yourself a slave.

Do you truly like yourself when you don't win?

How much of this is inside me?

How much . . .

. . . do I envy others for their success in sports, life, and relationships?

. . . do I concentrate on what I do not have?

. . . do I fear I am not good enough?

. . . am I fearful before a game or competition?

. . . do I love my opponent?

. . . do I reject God's love for me?

. . . do I believe that success is the ticket to becoming the person I want to be?

. . . do I like myself when I am losing?

. . . am I a slave to winning?

. . . do I feel that something is missing inside me?

The Consequences of Our Slavery

Once you have become a slave to the lies of the force of destruction, the enemy can use you to help him with his work. What is his work? To ruin God's plan for creation so he can prove that he is better than God. God made a world in which everything was good, and he put human beings in charge of it to safeguard this goodness. As long as human beings lived in agape love with God and each other, perfect peace reigned on earth. So the enemy decided to thwart God by getting human beings to bring about bad in the middle of God's good creation. The serpent's plan was to get Adam and Eve to compete with God. He wanted them to put their own wants ahead of God's command, because he knew their

> When you ignore or rebel against God, do you think you are helping the "force of destruction"?

rebellion would introduce self-centeredness into a previously God-centered world. For selfishness inevitably destroys peace by damaging relationships, causing hurt and harm. And that's just what their disobedience brought about:

Then the man and his wife heard the sound of the Lord
God as he was walking in the garden in the cool of the
day, and they hid from the Lord God among the trees of
the garden. But the Lord God called to the man, "Where
are you?" He answered, "I heard you in the garden, and
I was afraid because I was naked; so I hid." And he said,
"Who told you that you were naked? Have you eaten
from the tree that I commanded you not to eat from?" The
man said, "The woman you put here with me – she gave
me some fruit from the tree, and I ate it." Then the Lord
God said to the woman, "What is this you have done?"
The woman said, "The serpent deceived me, and I ate."
(Genesis 3:8–13)

Their rebellion damaged their relationship with God. Embarrassed by their foolishness and fearful of God's response, Adam and Eve hid from him when God came to take his usual walk with them. Their rebellion also damaged their relationship with each other. Adam and Eve had eaten the fruit to add to their self-worth. When things went bad, they naturally tried to make themselves still look as good as possible. When God asked Adam why he took a bite, he merely blamed the whole mess on his wife. So when God asked Eve why she did it, she simply blamed the snake. Both Adam and Eve had become slaves to making themselves look as good as possible apart from God. Sadly, their new need to look out for "number one" would never be satisfied, and it made it difficult to keep a good relationship with each other.

What things do we do to "cover up" our problems?

Since their nature was permanently changed, Adam and Eve passed their slavery to self-centeredness on to their children so that the whole human race has now inherited it. Let's look at the consequences for your life as a sportsperson today. Caught up in a futile search for self-worth apart from God, you focus your attention on getting what you need to achieve. And when you are worried about getting your own needs met, it's easy to overlook the needs of other people, even the needs of those closest to you. You can get so caught up in pursuing your goals that you take your loved ones for granted. You fail to see how your inattention hurts them, straining your relationship with them. In the end, you act off the court like basketball hogs do on the court. So driven to be the number one player on the team, these hot shots can only see openings where they can make a basket, not anyone else. And just as they aren't looking for ways to help their teammates to score, they're blind to how much their teammates resent them, regardless of how many points the hot shots contribute to a winning score. In pursuing your dreams, you can easily end up damaging your relationships. And when your actions hurt other people, you are doing the force of destruction's work.

> Have your sports goals taken priority over God or family? What are some ways our self-centeredness can cause us damage?

The Human Condition: Inner Conflict

In the end, we all have a war going on inside us. Even though we often put our needs first, we still long to live in love with others. The stupid selfish things we do not want to do, we often find ourselves doing. And the loving, giving things we want to do, we often don't do. No wonder we have a hard time understanding ourselves! Once again, the Bible accurately describes this war going on inside human nature: "I do not understand what I do. For what I want to do I do not do, but what I hate I do. I have the desire to do what is good, but I cannot carry it out. For what I do is not the good I want to do; no, the evil I do not want to do – this I keep on doing" (Romans 7:15, 18b–19). The ones we love, we often hurt. The ones who love us often do the same. This inner war breaks our hearts even as we break the hearts of others.

> How does your self-love get in the way of loving others?

Why does the meaning of life seem such a great mystery? Well, the honest answer is that it's hard to face ourselves, as another *Peanuts* cartoon illustrates. Lucy says to Charlie Brown, "You know what the whole trouble with you is Charlie Brown?", "No; and I don't want to know! Leave me alone!" As Charlie Brown walks away, Lucy shouts: "The whole trouble with you is you won't listen to what the whole trouble with you is!"[5] It's hard to face our inner war, so we simply try to not to think about it. We do have two sides. At times we can be very giving, but at other times we are clearly insensitive to the needs of others. It's far easier to look only at our good deeds, and try to ignore when we hurt others. But if we won't take a look at what is wrong with us, we condemn ourselves to never learning how to make things go right for us. For many people, life isn't one thing after another, but the same thing over and over.

> Are you honest with yourself about your own faults?

Those who refuse to look at their own shortcomings are condemned to live on a treadmill. They never find meaningful satisfaction. They only keep repeating their mistakes, over and over again.

But you don't have to. There is a better way.

WARNING
SIGNS

For we will all
stand before
God's judgment seat.
It is written:
"'As surely as I live,'
says the Lord,
,every knee
will bow before me;
every tongue will
confess to God.'"
So then, each of us
will give an account
of himself to God.

Romans 14:10b-12

Nothing in all of sport is more embarassing than scoring for your opponent. Just ask Jim Marshall of the Minnesota Vikings. Playing against San Francisco on October 25, 1964, Marshall picked up a fumble and ran the wrong way to score a two-point safety for the 49ers.[6] You've got to feel pretty foolish when you discover that you've gotten mixed up on the field and run the wrong direction. The goal you had hoped would help you now actually counts against you. It doesn't matter that it wasn't your intention. Just because you didn't understand what you were doing doesn't change the consequences. Rules are rules.

Life has its rules, too. As an athlete, you may like to think that you can make up your own, but it doesn't work that way. In football, players don't make the rules, the league officials do. And in life, human beings don't make up the rules, their Creator does. If you don't realize what his rules are, that doesn't change the fact that your actions will be judged by them. If you're running in the wrong direction, your actions will count against you, rather than for you, regardless of your intention.

Have you ever been in a situation where you were struggling against yourself, such as your workouts were hurting your performance? Have you ever reaped the consequences of an unintended action?

What are the rules? That we are to live in loving obedience to God and show agape love to one another. It's that simple.

In effect, God has designed life to be a team sport. To play at its best, a team needs to listen to its coach and get on well with each other. Good coaches bring out the best in their players while at the same time bringing them together into a cohesive unit. They teach their athletes the necessary sporting skills. Through correction and encouragement, they inspire their players to dig deeper than they knew they could, so that they find themselves able to perform at a higher level than they previously thought possible.

Good coaches also insist that the team work together. Their athletes always try to find ways to bring out the

Have you had any really good coaches in your sports career? What qualities made them special?

best performance in their teammates as well as themselves. Because each looks out for the other, one person's outstanding performance fires up his or her teammates to do their very best, and their good effort pumps up the first person who tries even harder to do well, which in turn reinforces the desire of the rest to keep trying hard, too. Despite the physical pain of giving it your all, all the players get an incredible mental high from performing at their best because they are working together. This mutual joy enables all the members of the team

to play together at a higher level than any of them could do on their own. In life, we need to look to God for guidance and encouragement so we can function at our full abilities. In life, we need to look out for our neighbor in love so we all can share the joy that makes us feel fully alive.

> What is easier, to love ourselves and our own dreams or to love God and others?

Life spent loving God and one another is that simple, and that hard. Because all human beings instinctively want to put themselves first, we often find it difficult to look out for others as much as ourselves. And when we act selfishly, we fall short of God's standard. The Bible calls these short-comings "sin" – a word which in Greek means "missing the mark," such as when you fail to hit the bull's eye on an archery target. Regardless of your intention, when you miss the mark, your actions count against you, not for you. That's because selfishness scores points for the force of destruction. And doing your enemy's work for him will bring about devastation in your life, even as he uses you to bring hurt and harm into the lives of others.

> As the Bible says, "Do not be deceived: God cannot be mocked. A man reaps what he sows. The one who sows to please his sinful nature, from that nature will reap destruction" (Galatians 6:8a).

> What do you think is more fun: team titles or individual titles?

Think again about a sports team. If everyone ignores the coach, each player will do whatever he or she thinks is best. There will be no team spirit. An outstanding performance by one player only leads to jealousy by the rest and a determination on their part to show that they are important, too. With everyone out to look good, teamwork goes out the window, plays just don't happen, and instead of pulling together to rally, the players do everything they can to make sure that they don't get blamed for the loss. No one takes risks to start something new. No one helps someone else when things go wrong. Frustrated and discouraged, all the members of the team play together at a poorer level than any of them could do on their own. At the game's end, they all lose.

> What selfish lies have you or someone you know bought into? Are the consequences always immediate? Are they physical, emotional, spiritual, or all three?

In life, as in sport, you become a loser when you live by listening to the selfish lies of sin. You run in the wrong direction. You score goals for the wrong team. You end up working hard for your own defeat.

The Consequences of Sin in this Life

Because God loves you, he wants to help you run in the right direction so that you can become a winner in life. That's why inside each of us, he has given us a conscience. God has written his rules for human beings on your heart, and your conscience reminds you of them. So your conscience acts as an internal coach, teaching you the best way to live by telling you whether something is the right or the wrong thing to do. If you listen to that inner voice, you will think of God and others as much as yourself, strengthening your relationship with both.

There's just one problem with this inner guidance system, however. You can choose to override it. And that's just what the force of destruction encourages you to do. He tries to get you to be self-centered and rebellious so you will run the opposite way from God's direction.

Selfishness. Sometimes you ignore your conscience so you can feel good at someone else's expense. Garrison Keillor shares a humorous example of this.

On this morning in August when I am thirteen, it's hot by ten o'clock. I poked along over the Post Toasties as long as I could, then my mother sent me out to pick tomatoes. [My brother and sister] were already out there . . . I threw a tomato at my brother. He whipped one back at me. We ducked down by the vines, heaving tomatoes at each other. My sister, who was a good person, said, "You're going to get it." She bent over and kept on picking. What a target! . . . Bending over, she looked like the side of a barn. I picked up a tomato so big it sat on the ground . . . It was very juicy . . . I stood up and took aim, and went into the wind-up, when my mother at the kitchen window called my name in a sharp voice. I had to decide quickly. I decided. A rotten Big Boy hitting the target is a memorable sound. Like a fat man doing a bellyflop, and followed by a whoop and a yell from the tomatoee.[7]

As told from Garrison Keillor's point-of-view, this story is funny. You can just imagine how good it must have felt, relieving his frustration at picking tomatoes by going into a great big wind-up and sending one flying at such a convenient target! Naturally, he doesn't mention the embarrassment his sister must have felt, the humiliation to have her fatness highlighted by his tomato, because that's not funny. You don't want to imagine how she felt. You enjoy his side of the story because you can identify with wanting to do what he did. We all learn early on to override our conscience's concern for the feelings of others when we want to make ourselves feel good.

> What sorts of things do you do to make yourself feel good that end up being at someone else's expense?

Rebellion. Sometimes, however, you ignore your conscience just because it appeals to the rebel inside of you. Nobody likes being told what to do, even if it's your own conscience that is reminding you of what is right. As descendants of Adam and Eve, deep down every person has a strong desire to be like God – the only one in all creation who doesn't have to answer to someone else. Sometimes you just want to show that no one has the right to tell you what to do. What better way can there be than doing just the opposite of what you're supposed to, just to prove you can? St. Augustine, a famous North African church leader, described his thrill in being a rebel back in AD 371.

Do you mind being told what to do? Does it depend upon who is telling you? What are the criteria to earn your obedience?

[When I was sixteen], there was a pear-tree near our vineyard, loaded with fruit which wasn't too tempting in looks or taste. Late one night, after finishing with sport, a bunch of us rowdies went over to shake down the tree and carry off the fruit . . . We took away an enormous amount, not so we could "pig-out," but just so we could throw it to pigs. Perhaps we ate some of the pears, but our real pleasure was in doing something that was forbidden.[8]

As this old story shows, athletes throughout the ages have always enjoyed trying to break the rules and not get caught.

What rebellious things have you done?

A Burned-Out Conscience. What happens when you override your conscience? If you keep it up, you will slowly burn it out. The first couple of times you do something you know you shouldn't do, you don't exactly feel good afterwards. Your conscience "bothers" you. Deep down, you know you've broken the rules written on your heart. You are embarrassed and sometimes even ashamed that you have failed to live up to being the kind of person you want to be and know you ought to be. To put it simply, you feel guilty.

Now, it is important to realize that not all guilt is the same.

Some people try to make you feel guilty as a way to get you to do things for them. That's just manipulation, and it's the flip-side of conditional love. People like that think you're worth loving only if you are doing whatever makes them happy. If

Have you been manipulated by guilt? Do you try to manipulate others with guilt? How is guilt from God different?

you do something that displeases them, they will try to make you feel worthless until you start doing what they want again. Guilt manipulation says you have no worth until you act to please someone else. The guilt that comes from God is the exact opposite. God-given guilt convicts you that you have failed to act in keeping with the worth God has been pleased to give you already when he made you in his image.

A conscience wounded by God-given guilt is painful. Why? To warn you that you are doing damage to yourself. Think about physical pain. The way you know that you have done something to a muscle during a game is the shooting pain. You may be able to play through with it hurting, but eventually you need to get it seen to properly. If you don't, you

Is God trying to warn you of something right now?

will permanently damage it. God designed physical pain to help you to know how to protect your body. God designed a guilty conscience to help you avoid destroying your inner person. You can "tough-out" God-given guilt, but only at your own peril.

If you ignore these guilt pangs long enough and keep doing what you know you shouldn't, you will short-circuit your conscience into silence. By persistently ignoring its warnings, you can sear your conscience as if with a hot iron, and in that area you don't feel anything again (1 Timothy 4:2).[9] Slavery to pleasing yourself wins your inner war on that specific issue.

You no longer remember God's rule. Without any sense of God's direction, you don't realize that you are doing anything wrong. You are simply doing something that now comes "naturally" to you.

> What small sins, if they continue, can later become natural for us?

A Burned-Out Life. Many people think a burned-out conscience means peace. After all, you no longer feel the tension of that inner conflict. You can do what you want relatively free from guilt. Thinking that way is as sensible as feeling free to forget about the oil in your engine when the dashboard light has stopped flashing because it has been on so long that it's burned out. Just because the driver mistakenly thinks there is no longer a problem doesn't mean that there isn't one. His actions are slowly burning up his engine whether he is aware of it or not. And now that the early warning light is out, nothing remains to tell him that he is destroying his engine until it is too late.

Just because one side has won the internal war doesn't necessarily mean that it's the right side. A conscience gone silent means serious damage has been to done to your inner person. If you let your desire to please yourself rule your life unopposed,

> What sins used to bother you when you did them but don't anymore?

you only score goals for the wrong team. Take relationships as an example. Without an active conscience to warn you, you fail to notice when you do hurtful things. So when other people back away from you, you don't understand why. Since you are just being "who you are," you don't change your ways. You simply press ahead, looking for a new relationship which you hope will work out better. When you break the rules of marriage to please yourself, you break the heart of your spouse and break up your family, causing yourself and those you love unspeakable pain. If you live this way long enough, you can easily end up lonely, with self-love only, seriously wounding your heart and those around you in the process.

The painful result of a broken heart is far worse than the prickings of a guilty conscience. If you break it too many times, your heart will lose the capacity to feel anything, just like your conscience. You won't feel pain any more, but you won't feel any joy either. For many people, the emptiness of no emotions still seems better than experiencing the on-going deep hurt of having continually sought love and always lost. Unfortunately, losing the capacity to feel also means losing the ability to love even yourself. And life without any love at all is not much of a life. Look at Kurt Cobain's song, "Dumb":

Have you known someone who couldn't feel pain or joy anymore?

> *My heart is broke*
> *But I have some glue*
> *Help me inhale*
> *And mend it with you*
> *We'll float around*
> *And hang out on clouds*
> *Then we'll come down*
> *And have a hangover . . . have a hangover* [10]

Cobain knew that a drug-induced emotional numbness wasn't a real answer for a hurting heart. The pain may be gone, but the emptiness hangs on like a hangover. Sadly, he concluded that the only way to end his pain and its hang-over was to take his own life. With Cobain's suicide, the lies of the force of destruction had finally finished their work in his life.

A silenced conscience may allow a pre-occupation with your own needs and desires to seem "natural." But if to be human means to give and to receive agape love, these "natural" actions only end up slowly destroying the very nature God gave you. If you continue to reject God's love and his guidance, you will eventually end up lost in life, a rebel without cause, a disappointed has-been without a clue.

How can some reject God yet nothing bad ever seems to happen to them? Do you think bad things eventually will happen to them?

The Eternal Consequences of a Burned-Out Conscience

Now the earth was corrupt in God's sight and was full of violence. God saw how corrupt the earth had become, for all the people on earth had corrupted their ways. So God said to Noah, "I am going to put an end to all people, for the earth is filled with violence because of them." (Genesis 6:11–13a)

The pain you feel from a conscience wounded by God-given guilt is a warning sign. Like Robot in the *Lost in Space* television series, a guilty conscience is shouting to you, "Danger, danger." If you persist in acting like this, you will burn yourself out, destroying your ability to feel good about yourself and other people. There is, however, another, far more serious danger awaiting you. If you consistently reject God's love and guidance, you will be cut off from Him forever.

Eternal Separation. If a player is having trouble with his conduct both on and off the field, a good coach will be patient

What do you think will happen to us when we die? Why would you expect to enter Heaven?

and try to help him get his act together. But if the player never quite gets with the program, there will come a point when, for the good of the rest of the team, the coach will be forced to cut him from the roster.

What does a good coach do about a bad player?

God is in a similar situation with humanity. A loving, all-powerful Creator cannot permit human beings to misuse their gifts and hurt one another indefinitely. There must come a point when he says, "No more!" A loving, all-powerful God must eventually separate those who rebel against his rules and hurt other people from those who do not. Otherwise, those who follow the rules will never be able to live in peace and joy with God and each other.

Such a point came during Noah's days. Noah was a man who did right and walked with God, but he was surrounded by people whose "every inclination of the thoughts of [their] heart was only evil all the time" (Genesis 6:5). God decided to free the world from the extreme depth of violence into which it had sunk. He flooded the earth, destroying everyone but Noah and his family.

Would you want a disruptive player on your team? What if you were the disruptive player?

The Flood, however, didn't permanently solve the problem of human selfishness. Noah trusted God and obeyed his command to build the ark (Hebrews 11:7), but he was still a descendent of Adam and Eve. He had inherited from them an imperfect nature and so passed on to his descendants humanity's problem with rebellious self-pleasing. That's why today you still see all the suffering and pain which human beings inflict on one another.

But the story of the flood stands as a warning. One day in the future, God will decide enough is finally enough. He will destroy once and for all time the force of destruction and all destructive self-serving among people. On that day, God will call everyone to give an account of his or her life. He will examine whether we have done good with the gifts and talents he has entrusted to us. He will also openly display

> Do you believe that people basically are giving or self-centered?

what hurt and harm we have caused others during our lifetime. God will then judge us, punishing every wrong and rewarding every good. He will decide who should be spared and who should be swept away, who should live with him forever and who should go away to eternal separation from his presence. What happens to us if we should die before that great reckoning day when God will rid the world of all evil? We undergo judgment right then. Depending on his decision, either we enter immediately into God's eternal presence or into the place of his eternal absence.

In effect, Judgment Day will be something like what British soccer officials do with important matches. They film their games so that afterwards they can review the videotape for any evidence of rule breaking. If they spot an infraction which the referee didn't see during the match, the officials assess penalties at that time, even though the game is over. The job of these officials is to make sure that no wrong-doing goes unpunished.

It's easy to think that if you're clever and fast, you can break the rules and not get caught. The Bible, however, warns what the truth is. Even if you somehow manage to fool other people in this life, you won't get away with your wrong-doing forever. When you die, God will roll the videotape of everything you have ever done in your life and pass judgment on you. Individuals who failed to get with God's program during their lives will find that their names have been cut from the roster of those who will be on God's team forever.

Heaven and Hell. The Bible calls the place where God is "Heaven" and the place where people live apart from him forever "Hell." What are they like? Heaven is the place where God wipes away every tear, works every earthly wrong to an eternal right, and enables humanity to live in agape love with him and each other all the time. The Bible describes Heaven like this:

> *"Now the dwelling of God is with men, and he will live with them. They will be his people, and God himself will be with them and be their God. He will wipe every tear from their eyes. There will be no more death or mourning or crying or pain, for the old order of things has passed away"* (Revelation 21: 3–4).

So Heaven is the place where God receives his proper honor, and humanity can at last live in perfect love, finding permanent fulfillment and value, forever.

> If you were given a choice, would you choose Heaven or Hell? What do you think heaven is like?

What is Hell like? Jesus called it a place of darkness and eternal punishment, where there is weeping and gnashing of teeth (Matthew 25:30, 46). Who can think of a punishment more painful than to spend eternity in a place where nothing is honored but self? To find yourself forever trying to find satisfaction for yourself from equally self-pleasing people always looking for you to satisfy them – what an awful eternal fate! Living for all eternity in the midst of permanent self-centeredness can only mean constant dissatisfaction and sorrow. The Bible describes this fate as being thrown into a "fiery lake of burning sulfur" (Revelation 21:8).

Ann Landers retells an old story which illustrates the fundamentally different character of the people in Heaven and Hell:

> *A man spoke with the Lord about heaven and hell. The Lord said to the man, "Come, I will show you hell." They entered a room where a group of people sat around a huge pot of stew. Everyone was famished, desperate and starving. Each held a spoon that reached the pot, but each spoon had a handle so much longer than their own arm that it could not be used to get the stew into their own mouths. The suffering was terrible. "Come, now I will show you heaven," the Lord said after a while. They entered another room, identical to the first – the pot of stew, the group of people, the same long-handled spoons. But there everyone was happy and well-nourished. "I don't understand," said the man. "Why are they happy here when they were miserable in the other room and everything was the same?" The Lord smiled. "Ah, it is simple," he said. "Here they have learned to feed each other."[11]*

Summary of the Human Situation

The penalty for sin is death – eternal exile from God's world and his presence (Romans 6:23). Those who reject God and his guidance, even if only from time to time, will suffer permanent separation from Him forever. After all, if people who only occasionally hurt others through their self-centeredness are permitted into Heaven, Heaven won't be that much different from life in this world. And if Heaven isn't really any different from life as we know it now, what's the point? No, no one with any amount of selfishness within will be permitted to enter Heaven. Only those who have always shown agape love to God and other people will experience the joys of permanent peace and satisfaction in God's eternal presence.

What would make a loving God send people to Hell?

Of course, all human beings are selfish to some degree. That's why we all are guilty of falling short of God's standard for his creation (Romans 3:23). As a result, we all stand under the threat of death and eternal punishment. To escape the coming judgment, you need two things. First, you need to make up for all the wrongs you have done. Second, you need to change your nature and prepare yourself to fit into a place where everyone lives by agape love alone. But you say, "No one can possibly fulfill either one of those requirements." That's right!

But you don't have to. There is a better way.

THE SAVING WORK OF JESUS CHRIST

A cartoon by Gary Larson of *The Far Side* shows a student trying to go through the front door of the Midvale School for the Intellectually Gifted. Head down, he pushes with all his might, never seeing a big sign on the door which reads "Pull."

It's easy for athletes to make the same mistake. The pace of your life is fast and filled with constant activities. Daily training, regular traveling, constant monitoring of what you eat – surely an hour doesn't go by that you're not thinking about how what you're doing now is going to affect your success in competition. And then there are the pressures – pressure to win and keep winning, pressure to please your family and friends, pressure to make yourself a somebody, pressure to understand yourself and make other people understand you as well. It's enough to make you want to block it all out, to survive competitive sports by simply putting your head down and trying to push aside everything

For God so loved
the world
that he gave
his one and only Son,
that whoever
believes in him
shall not perish
but have
eternal life.

John 3:16

that gets in your way.

But the door to joy won't open that way. And when you grow tired of the door refusing to budge, it's time to stop pushing, look up, and read the sign. What does the sign say? It simply reads "Jesus." You don't have to try to pry open the door to joy. Jesus will open it for you, because Jesus is the better way.

The Bible tells us that Jesus is God Almighty come to earth as a human being. History is filled with human beings who wanted to be God, but only one God who wanted to be human. Why did God want to become human? So he could in person call us back to a relationship with himself and make that relationship possible. Jesus told the people of his day that he was the true source of joy: "I have come that they may have life, and have it to the full" (John 10:10b). He warned them that they could easily pursue accomplishments but end-up empty-handed on the Day of Judgment: "What good will it be for a man if he gains the whole world, yet forfeits his soul?" (Matthew 16:26) He offered help to those tired of pushing against doors that wouldn't budge: "Come to me, all you who are weary and burdened, and I will give you rest. Take my yoke upon you and learn from me, for I am gentle and humble in heart, and you will find rest for your souls" (Matthew 11:28–9). He even offered hope to those separated from God because of their sin: He said, "Your sins are forgiven" (Mark 2:5b). So Jesus is more than just a great moral teacher. Jesus claims to be the only one who can solve our greatest problem in life: "I am the way and the truth and the life. No one comes to the

> History is filled with human beings who wanted to be God, but only one God who wanted to be human.

Father except through me" (John 14:6). His followers recorded his teachings for future generations so that, through the Bible,

Jesus can show us how he will reunite us with our Maker today.

That's good news, because just deciding that we want a relationship with God doesn't mean that it can happen automatically. Suppose a football team has fallen behind their opponents because the players have been arguing among themselves. They don't just automatically take the lead in the game when they wake up and start pulling together. The score has to change before they can be declared the winners. Even once we realize that we need God in our lives, the sins on our scorecard mean

How did your scorecard read before you realized that you needed God? How does it read now?

we are still under a sentence of death and eternal separation from God. Only Jesus' saving work on the cross can change our scorecard in God's eyes.

The Problem of Sin

Our sinful scorecard presents God with a really difficult problem. If he gives us our just deserts, he has lost a relationship with us forever – the very purpose for which his love created us. Yet, if God simply chooses to overlook our guilt when we want to come back, he destroys the very basis

on which we are able to have a relationship with him. That's because to have a good relationship, you need to understand yourself, understand the other person, and agree on how you are to get along. A relationship with God isn't any different. If he ignored our sin, we would develop a distorted view of who we are, who he is, and how we are to relate to each other.

Are we doing somebody a favor if we're easy on violations of the rules? What if our parents never disciplined us or showed us "tough love"?

Think about it. A basketball coach establishes clear training rules, including an early curfew during tournaments on the road. Any violators will be benched during the next game. After winning the first game, the star center misses curfew by a half hour because he has been celebrating with his girlfriend who drove up to watch.

The coach finds out. The next game in the tournament is against the school's cross-town rivals. The guilty athlete is really apologetic and wants to do his part for the team in the big game. What will a good coach do? He'll still bench the star athlete. Why? He will want to make sure that there is no more "failure to communicate." He will want to make sure that his player really understands some things.

> Have you ever been in a situation where a coach needed to discipline you? Did he do it? Are you glad he did?

God punishes sin for the same reason. Let's compare the two situations.

Understanding Ourselves

■ First, the star athlete needs to learn something about himself. No matter how good he thinks he is, he is not above the rules. When he breaks the rules, he's not proving that he's special, just that he's selfish. Nothing will communicate these hard truths to the wayward player better than watching his team lose while he is sitting on the bench.

■ Human beings need to learn that they aren't their own boss like God. If God didn't punish our sin, we would never have to face the truth that we aren't above his rules. We would never see our self-centeredness for what it is.

Understanding God

■ Second, the basketball player needs to understand his coach better. He broke the rules because he didn't think that the coach would take his violations seriously. The star athlete needs to understand how deeply the coach hates it when players refuse to prepare for games properly.

■ He also needs to understand that his coach is fair. It wouldn't be right for the wayward player to get off scot free after enjoying something that the other players had obediently given up. Since he stole some prohibited pleasure, it is only right and fair that he experience some pain as a just punishment.

■ Finally, the basketball player has challenged the authority of the coach to set the rules. If the coach does not exact a consequence for disobedience, then he will be signaling all his players that he doesn't take his authority as coach very seriously, and neither do they need to. By making the star player sit on the bench, the coach clearly communicates how much he values proper training, how determined he is to treat everyone equally, and how firm he is in his authority.

■ God's punishment of sin also helps us understand him better. The Bible tell us God is a holy God. That means in him, there is no selfishness, no injustice – just pure power acting in pure love. God must punish sin because he detests self-serving and all the hurt it brings to the creatures he loves. Refusing to punish wrong-doing would mean that God didn't really care about the suffering of the people who had been wronged.

■ God also must punish sin because he is just. He has created the universe according to unchangeable principles of right and wrong, as our conscience and the Bible remind us. Simple fairness requires that those who do right are rewarded and that those who do wrong are punished.

■ Finally, God must punish sin because he is God. He has made the rules for everyone's benefit. It's his job to use his authority and power to make sure that everybody lives by them. Consequently, at the time of judgment, there will be a separation between those who live by agape love and those who live for themselves. Those through whom God's perfect love flows will know eternal peace. But those whose self-seeking has made them slaves to the force destruction, they will experience eternal punishment. For pure power acting in pure love must hate and seek to destroy all selfishness and injustice. Describing the holiness of God, the Bible says that "Our 'God is a consuming fire'" (Hebrews 12:29). His love will burn up everything that is not already afire with agape love. By punishing sin with a penalty as severe as death, God helps us understand how completely impossible it is for him to tolerate self-centeredness in his holy presence.

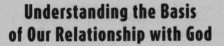

Understanding the Basis
of Our Relationship with God

■ The third lesson the basketball player needs to learn is the importance of trust. As the Bible says, how can two people walk together unless they agree? (Amos 3:3) The athlete and his coach can have a good working relationship only if they trust each other. The player has to trust the wisdom of the coach's methods and the judgment of his decisions. The coach has to trust that his players will listen to what he says and do it with all their heart. If there isn't trust between coach and players, nothing will happen but losing on court followed by bickering and back-biting off of it. By benching the star athlete, the coach is making it clear that if he can't trust you, he won't play you.

■ God wants our relationship to be based on love, and love requires trust. Because of who God is, we can trust that his love is firmly fixed on us. But from the very beginning the force of destruction has been at work to make us doubt God's trustworthiness. When we do, we feel free to rebel. We fail to fix our love firmly on God, becoming untrustworthy ourselves as a result. God punishes sin with a penalty as severe as death to show that if he can't trust us to live only by agape love, we can't play a part in his eternal kingdom.

So, human sin presents God with a really difficult problem. He must punish our wrong-doing with death. But when he does, he forfeits forever having the relationship with us for which he created us. Adam and Eve, you and I, we all have put God in a "Catch-22" predicament. Either way God goes, choosing to punish us or choosing to ignore our sins, he loses something important to who he is and to his relationship with us. That's the reality of the situation, unless some way can be found for the punishment to be paid by someone else on our behalf. If God must punish sin with death, but doesn't want us to have to pay that price, we need to find someone who can and will pay that price so we don't have to.

Take the example of the star basketball player. Let's change the story a little. Say that two brothers are battling for the starting position as centers, Jake Houltberg who is a senior and Cal Houltberg who is a junior. Although really close, they are fiercely competitive with each other. So far this season, the coach has gone back and forth between them, but for the tournament he has decided to start Jake. After the first night of the tournament, Jake stays out a half hour after curfew with his girlfriend. Out of the corner of his eye, the coach sees a Houltberg sneaking into their hotel room. But the coach isn't sure whether it was Jake or Cal. The next morning he confronts the brothers at breakfast.

"Boys, I saw one of you coming in after curfew last night. I couldn't tell which one, but from the blond hair, I knew it had to be a Houltberg. I'm really sorry to have to do this, but you know the rules. Now which one of my star centers am I going to have to bench for the biggest game of the year?"

Before Jake can open his mouth, Cal speaks out, "Coach, I know the rules, and I'll take responsibility for breaking curfew."

After the coach leaves, Jake turns to Cal and says, "Why did you lie for me?"

"I didn't lie," Cal says with a big smile. "Coach asked which of us he was going to bench. I volunteered. I do know the rules, and I am willing to take responsibility for you breaking curfew."

"You didn't have to."

"I know. What you did last night was really stupid, but Mom and Dad are so looking forward to cheering for you today, I couldn't stand to see their hearts broken like that. And to tell you the truth, I couldn't stand to see the high point of your senior season go down the drain because you got a little carried away last night. I'll get my turn next year."

"But, this is your big chance, and I was the one who was guilty," protests Jake. "I don't deserve to get to play."

"So what else is a brother for?"

Although Cal naturally wanted to play in the big game of the year, out of love for his family he had offered himself as a substitute for his brother. He freely chose to assume responsibility for Jake's actions so Jake wouldn't have to. Cal's sitting on the bench during the game made clear to everyone that there was a high price to pay for breaking the rules. Justice was served. But the light in Jake's eyes and the joy on his parents' face made Cal's personal pain all seem worthwhile. Knowing that he had no right to be there, Jake played his heart out. He put on the best performance of his career, because that night he was motivated not by personal pride, but by loving gratitude.

Before the beginning of time, God saw way into the future that Adam, Eve, you, and I would all put him in this "Catch-22."

> Have you ever had someone take the blame for your wrong? Have you ever taken the blame for someone else? How did it feel?

So he devised a substitution strategy to take care of the problem even before he created human beings. And he designed his substitution plan to be a really good learning experience for humanity. He decided to use the problem of sin to show us the true meaning of his agape love. It's in looking at God's substitution strategy that we see how much he loves us and how much he wants us to love him in return.

Christ Our Substitute

Here is a trustworthy saying that deserves full acceptance: Christ Jesus came into the world to save sinners. (1 Timothy 1:15)

What is God's substitution plan? God needed someone who was human. The substitute had to be flesh and blood, subject to the same temptations we have and, therefore, subject to the same penalty of death if he disobeyed. But all human beings after Adam and Eve are born with an imperfect nature that makes it inevitable that they will seek to honor themselves more than God. Who could he find who bore his image but was without sin? Only God himself met those requirements. So God decided to do the unthinkable. He decided that he would become human. He would substitute himself for humanity and take our punishment on himself. That way justice would be served and such a wondrous display of agape love would move humanity to return with loving gratitude to their Maker.

> It's in looking at God's substitution strategy that we see how much he loves us and how much he wants us to love him in return.

How could it be possible for God to become human? Well,

obviously that's hard to describe to the last detail. It's true that God can do anything he wants to. By definition, that's what it means to be God Almighty. But to help us understand how it happened, God has given us an outline.

Now God is such an incredible being, that within himself there are three different persons – God the Father, God the Son, and God the Holy Spirit. Christians have a name for this mystery of multiple persons within God. They call it the Trinity. The word is a shortened form of "tri-unity," or "Three-in-One." You can't fully explain a mystery like the Trinity, or else it wouldn't be a mystery! The best you can do is compare it to things we do understand. St. Patrick explained the Trinity to the Irish by comparing God to a three-leaf clover. God the

Father, God the Son, and God the Holy Spirit were each a separate petal. But each leaf was still part of the same piece of clover. God the Father, God the Son, and God the Holy Spirit were each equally divine but still united together as one God.

Another way to look at the Trinity is as if it were one sports team with three equal players, each responsible for a different position. The Father is the source of all, who oversees the universe from heaven. The Son is God showing himself to humankind as their savior. He normally lives with the Father in Heaven but was sent to live on earth for a time. And the Holy Spirit is God's constant presence on earth.

When it came time to present a substitute for humanity, God the Father sent God the Son down from Heaven to be born of a young woman named Mary through the work of God the Holy Spirit. At birth, he was given the name Jesus, which means "The LORD saves." Like his Father he is fully God, and like his mother he is fully human. According to the Bible, during his earthly life Jesus was "tempted in every way, just as we are – yet was without sin" (Hebrews 4:15b). Therefore, he is the perfect substitute for all humanity.

> Why do you think that most people totally miss God's substitution plan? What are some of the reasons people don't accept Jesus' substitution for them?

Jesus came into the world not only to tell us we need to return to God but also to make that possible. He knew the rules, and he knew humanity had broken them. He knew the penalty that had to be paid and that only he could pay it. He knew what great things would be in store for us if that penalty was paid on our behalf. And he knew how heartbroken God would be to lose our love for eternity. The best-selling novel *The Christmas Box* points this out. We all know how indescribably awful it is for a parent to lose a child. How much more, then, must God

grieve at the eternal loss of even one of his children? Because Jesus loves the Father and loves us, he freely chose to assume responsibility for our sin and shoulder the consequences. Therefore, although he himself was fully God in his own right, he humbly submitted himself to death, even to a death as awful as on a cross.

Jesus came into the world not only to tell us we need to return to God but also to make that possible.

To appreciate fully what Jesus did for us it is necessary to know something about crucifixion. The Romans devised this method of execution to be an instrument of death by torture. They wanted this punishment to be so notoriously cruel that no one would dare revolt against their rule. The nails in Jesus' hands and feet didn't kill him, nor did the spear in his side. The real cause of his death was far more horrible. Just try to imagine what it was like. Crucifixion kills you by slow suffocation. Before the Romans would put you on the cross they whipped your back so that fluids would flood your lungs, making it difficult for you to breathe. When they hoisted you up in the air, your arms would be stretched above your head. As a result, your diaphragm could not expand unless you pushed your body up with your thigh muscles. After a while those muscles would get tired, and you would get charley horses. You would then slump back until you couldn't stand not breathing any more. Then the only way to get a gulp of air would be to force those muscles in spasm to push up yet again. At which point your body began to rock back and forth between the terror of not being able to breathe and the intense pain of pushing up your body with muscles in spasm. This awful rhythm continued until you couldn't stand the charley horses in your thighs and you let yourself suffocate.

And yet, as awful as such a death is, nothing could have

been more painful for Jesus than being separated from God the Father. On the cross Jesus quotes the beginning of Psalm 22: "My God, my God, why have you forsaken me?" (Mark 15:34b) No doubt he did so to refer to the whole psalm, not just its opening line, for it tells the story of someone undergoing intense suffering who praises God for his eventual vindication (Psalm 22:22-24).[12] Nevertheless, this verse accurately describes what Jesus was experiencing at that moment on the cross. Although he himself had committed no sin, on the cross Jesus shouldered the sins of the whole world (2 Corinthians 5:21).[13] Bearing all our sins, he could at that point no longer sense the Father's presence. Surely, the separation of Jesus from God the Father was a punishment so infinitely severe that his substitution for us more than paid in full the debt humanity owed for all the sins of the world. Because Jesus paid the full penalty for our rule-breaking, we can have a fresh start with God.

Therefore, the cross of Christ clearly displays the full character of the God who loves us. Here his justice and his mercy meet. Jesus'

"Jesus Christ is the atoning sacrifice for our sins, and not only for ours but also for the sins of the hole world." (1 John 2:2)

death and separation from God while on the cross satisfied God's concern for justice. That he suffered death so we don't have to satisfied God's desire for mercy. On the cross Jesus himself asked that God would forgive those who crucified him (Luke 23:34). His own words confirmed that his crucifixion had made such forgiveness possible. Right before he died, Jesus said, "It is finished" (John 19:30a). The Savior of the world was willing to have his hands nailed to a cross so that everyone could come within his loving embrace.

Do you ever wonder why Jesus is the most celebrated person in history?

The Cross of Christ:
The Sure Sign that God Loves You

As we discussed in Chapter 2, it's easy to fall into the trap of feeling that you have to earn the approval of others, whether it's your father's respect, your coach's confidence, the cheers of the crowd, or the affection of someone special. In each case, you try to figure out what they are looking for, and then do your best to fit the bill. It's not surprising, then, that many people feel that they have to earn God's love, too. They mistakenly reason like this. Since God is perfectly good, if you want his approval you must first show him how really, really good you are. If you aren't good like God, you have no business bothering him in the first place. You'd just be acting like a hypocrite.

The cross of Christ proves to us that God doesn't think that way at all. The cross reminds us that no one can be good enough to earn God's approval. Being descendants of Adam and Eve, we all fall short of God's perfect standard. If we could meet God's standard by trying hard enough, Jesus would not have had to die. As important, the cross also shows us that no one has to try to be good enough to prove to God that we are worthy of his love. Centuries and centuries before we were born, God clearly showed his love for us by dying in our place on the cross. Long before we could even try to prove our love for God, God had already proved his love for us.

Yet, even if we don't need to try to earn God's approval, we often expect God to earn ours. We all like it when other people show that they appreciate us, whether

Do you feel that you have to clean up before you can go before God? Do you sometimes think you need to do more to earn God's forgiveness?

it's a compliment from the coach, a great Christmas present from our parents, or just a letter or phone call from someone special when we are on the road. It makes us feel good to receive a concrete reminder that somebody really cares about us. It's only natural, then, that we would like God to do the same for us. Many people argue that they would believe in God, if only he would just do something to prove to them that he really is there and really does care.

Do you ever wish God would do more for you?

Some people would like God to prove his love by answering an important prayer the way they want. What athlete hasn't at one time or another sent a stray prayer up to Heaven in a tough situation? Who hasn't promised to give God a chance, if he would come through just this once? But when things don't work out they way they hope, people become disillusioned. They say, "If God was really there and really did care, he would have done what I asked.

He knew how badly I wanted it, and what a good thing it would have been, if it had happened." Others want God to prove that he loves them by giving them some kind of miraculous sign or letting them in on some mysterious ancient secret. They become disappointed when God fails to speak to them in an audible voice or give them a vision of Heaven or impart to them some mystical power. Still others want God to make this a perfect world to show that he really is there and cares. They look at all the suffering and evil on earth and say that God can't exist, or, if he does, he doesn't do much good for us down here.

Like that student at Midvale School for the Intellectually Gifted, these people have put their head down and become frustrated that they were not able to push open the door to a relationship with God. If they would only look up at the cross, they would see how his love displayed there answers all their questions. Some want God to give them something to prove his love. What more could God give than his very life to show the depth of his love? Others want a miraculous appearance or an ancient mystery about God. What could be more miraculous than God himself coming into this world in the flesh or more mysterious than the Immortal One being willing to die at the hands of those he had made? Still others demand that God have compassion on the suffering by ridding the world of evil. Who could have more compassion for the abused than Jesus who himself was whipped, mocked, spat on, and then finally crucified? What could be a surer sign that God will one day destroy all destructive forces in the world than this, that God condemned his own Son to death because

> Have you ever questioned God's existence or his goodness?

> Is there an issue or question that is keeping you from accepting that God is powerful and loving?

Jesus took responsibility for the sins of the world?

When you look up to the cross of Christ, you see how God's love has pulled open the door for you. Now you can walk through and have a relationship with him. Jesus on the cross offers you a glorious exchange. He says, "As God's Son, I have a special, close relationship with God the Father. He will raise me from the dead, and I get to live with him for all eternity. As a human being, your sins prevent you from knowing God's love in your heart now. And when you die, you will be eternally separated from him forever. Why don't we trade? If you will give me your sins, I will give you my relationship with the Father. Because of me, God will forgive all your sins, adopt you as his own child, put the assurance of his agape love in your heart,

> When Christians look to the cross of Christ, they see God's concrete assurance that they have a permanent place in his family, now and forever.

help you to become the very best you can be, and bring you to live with him forever when you die." When Christians look to the cross of Christ, they see clear proof that God really does love them and has good plans for their future.

Today, the cross of Christ is a popular symbol. Ministers walk behind them to go in and out of a religious service. Churches have them on top of steeples so you can see them from miles away. Countries have them on their flags for all the world to see. Even pop stars wear them around their necks or pierced in the ear. No one in the ancient world would have done that. In the Roman Empire, the cross was a symbol of suffering and shame because only the very worst criminals were executed that way. Wearing a cross around your neck back then would have been like wearing a hangman's noose or an electric chair today. What brought about such a remarkable change in attitude? Christ's death on a cross made it a symbol of certain hope for generations of people. Today, when Christians look at the cross, they see God's concrete assurance that they have a permanent place in his family, now and forever. What do you see?

CHRIST OUR NEW LIFE

CHAPTER 5

I will sprinkle
clean water on you,
and you will be clean;
I will cleanse you
from all your impurities
and from all your idols.
I will give you
a new heart
and put a new spirit
in you;
I will remove from you
your heart of stone
and give you
a heart of flesh.
And I will put
my Spirit in you
and move you
to follow my decrees
and be careful
to keep my laws . . .
You will be my people,
and I will be your God.

Ezekiel 36:25-28

Nothing in sport is as exciting as watching a dramatic comeback. It gets you on the edge of your seat to see the team you had given up all hope of winning suddenly begin to turn things around at the last minute. The tension builds as each point brings them closer to going ahead, while each passing second means less time to do it in. Soon, you find yourself thinking, "They might just do it, but can they? It looks like they're going to do it, but I don't know, it's going to be tough. Wait, this might be it." When they score the winning goal right as time runs out, you leap up cheering wildly. You can't believe what you've just seen, but you know it's true. Your team has managed to pull out a victory from the jaws of certain defeat. All that disappointment you were dreading because you knew they were going to lose is instantly swallowed up in the euphoria of a victory made all the sweeter because it was so unexpected.

In the eyes of his followers,

Jesus made a similarly unexpected, if far more spectacular, comeback. When Jesus was crucified, his followers thought all hope was lost. Like so many people today, they did not understand why Jesus had to die.

> Have you ever been a part of an exciting comeback? Have you watched one happen while you were on the other team?

They had hoped he was the one God had promised to send to make all things right in this world. And yet, when his broken body was taken down for burial, Jesus was clearly dead, and nothing in this world had seemed to change at all. His humiliating death on the cross seemed irreversible proof that his mission had failed.

But, three days later on Easter morning, his followers heard disturbing reports that his tomb was empty. Some women claimed that an angel had told them that Jesus had risen from the dead. Most thought their story was nonsense, but some wondered if it might just be possible. That evening his followers were debating among themselves about the confusing events of the day, when Jesus amazed them all. Although his followers had seen him dead, against all the laws of nature, there he was, fully alive again and standing in their midst. Something had happened on the cross after all, and of far greater importance than they could have ever imagined. By paying the price for sin, Jesus had defeated death itself – the ultimate work of the force of destruction, the final consequence of sin. His followers' joy knew no bounds. The Lord they knew and loved could once again walk with them, talk with them, and be a part of their daily life.

Forty days later, the risen Jesus was taken up into heaven where he now sits at the right hand of God the Father, praying for us at all times. But being freed from the laws of nature by his resurrection, Jesus promised to continue to be spiritually present with his followers. Wherever they went, Jesus was there with each one, even when they split up and went different directions. Eventually, they all died and went on to eternal life in Heaven. But Jesus, having conquered death in this world, continued to stay and be a spiritual part of the daily lives of the people his followers had introduced him to.

That's why when Christians today talk about Jesus Christ, they are not just talking about a historical figure who lived and died 2000 years ago like Julius Caesar or Cleopatra. They're talking about someone who is alive right now. Stop and think about it. With every other important person from the past, no matter how much you study their lives, you can never interact with them like you do with the people around you right now. You can admire Babe Ruth. You can read all about his life story and learn his stats by heart. You can even spend lots of money collecting memorabilia of his career. But no matter how hard you try, in this life you will never get to know him as a friend or have him as your coach. Jesus is different. Because of his resurrection, Jesus is able to be a

> What historical figure would you most want to meet? What would you do if you were to meet Jesus?

> How would you feel if Jesus were to know you like your best friend does?

part of everyone's daily life, whether you live in Beijing, China, Kampala, Uganda, Salina, Kansas or Edinburgh, Scotland.

Although Christianity has rules like loving God and other people, Christianity isn't about following rules. Although it has rituals like reading the Bible and going to church regularly, Christianity isn't about rituals. Because of the resurrection of Jesus Christ, Christianity is all about having a relationship with a living, loving God. Not rules, not rituals, but a relationship – that's what Jesus' resurrection makes possible. You really can know God personally today. You really can ask him questions and hear him give you guidance. You really can enjoy spending time with him and know the good feeling when he is really pleased with you. But above everything else, you really can experience him changing your life for the better, so you can become the best you can be!

How does having a regular relationship with Jesus change your life? He does for you what even your best friend or greatest coach cannot do. He undoes what the force of destruction has done in you. As Jesus said, "The thief comes only to steal and kill and destroy; I have come that they may have life, and have it to the full" (John 10:10).

The force of destruction worms its way into your heart, distracting you from God's love and entangling you in self-defeating ways. The aim of sin is to steal your God-given potential, to kill your joy and to deaden your ability to love.

> Do you think you will ever fulfill all of your God-given potential?

In the end, your enemy seeks to destroy you with death in this life and to snare you into deserving to share his fate of eternal punishment in the next.

But Jesus came to give you life to the full. His resurrection from the dead proves that he has the power to reverse the results of the force of destruction's work in this world. Through Jesus, you can be cleansed from your sin, given a new

> For those who have turned to him, Jesus returns what sin has stolen from them.

ability to love by the power of God's Spirit in you, and made permanently a part of God's family. For those who have turned to him, Jesus returns what sin has stolen from them.

Conversion

Turn us back to you, O LORD, that we may return. (Lamentations 5:21)[14]

G od created human beings to have a love relationship with him. And love requires trust. So God's plan for rescuing humanity from sin is based on trust. To have a permanent relationship with God you must believe his promises to you, rather than rely on your own efforts to prove you're good enough to be with God. After all, if you could buy your salvation through your good conduct, getting to know God would just be a business transaction. But you don't have it in you to be good enough. And, besides, God wants even more than your good conduct. He wants your love, too. So God designed his rescue plan to be a free gift, knowing that as you come to trust in what his great love has made possible, you will naturally come to love him in return. That's why a relationship with God is based on faith in God's promises. So you will learn to love him as much as he loves you.

As the first step toward this love relationship, Jesus sends the Holy Spirit to work in our lives. We need his help. We've spent so many years listening to the lies of the force of destruction that our hearts are hard toward God. We don't even listen to what he has to say, let alone trust what he says. We've developed a mindset that is hostile to God, because we've gotten used to doing things our own way. So we don't want to start submitting to God's way now. That would be like a new coach arriving on the scene and telling professional athletes that their grasp of the basics was so fundamentally flawed that they would have

How do you respond to change in your life?

to start over from scratch and change their whole approach. It's unlikely that at that point in their career the athletes could change, even if they wanted to. And, of course, we don't have it in us to follow God's way, even if we really tried. So we push God and his truth away. We ignore the Bible and our conscience and set up standards that make us think we're doing okay without God.

> Even though a particular change can be very difficult, do you feel that it can become something good?

We know that our lives are not perfect. We realize that we've done some things we'd just as soon forget. But we still feel that we have done a lot of other things we really can be proud of. We may not be the perfect person, but we still feel confident that we're not as bad as some folks we know, and maybe even better than many. If there really is a God, we tell ourselves, we'll be okay when we die. God will have to let us into Heaven, because we're basically just as good and decent as most everyone else. But the truth is, no one is good enough to deserve to go to Heaven (Romans 8:7–8).[15]

If getting right with God were left up to human beings to start the process, we would never begin. We are too comfortable being in charge of our lives, no matter how unhappy we may be. Even when faced with the destruction that sin has worked in our lives, we find it more natural to blame our problems on everyone or everything else rather than on the power of sin working in us. When athletes have problems with coaches, officials, agents, competitors, family, friends, special friends, the public – you name it – their own self-centeredness never seems to be a factor. Seeing sin for what it is is beyond humanity. And if we don't see our sin, we'll never go looking for a Savior. The British evangelist John Stott has written, "Nothing keeps people away from

Christ more than their inability to see their need of him or their unwillingness to admit it."[16] The number one work of the power of sin is to blind us to our need of God and keep us from admitting it.

Jesus knew that humanity would never realize their need for God on their own. So he promised his disciples that after his

> In the game of life, how are you playing? Do you sense a personal need to have forgiveness?

resurrection he would send God the Holy Spirit to guide the world into all truth. Now the same power that restored Jesus to life is at work in this world to draw people back to God. Working through the Bible whose writers he inspired, the Holy Spirit makes us aware of our need of God and his great desire to have us return to him. The first work of the Holy Spirit is to help us overcome our hostility toward God so we can see ourselves and God in a new light.

As we read in the Bible about his plan to rescue us, the Holy Spirit turns our hearts back to God. He opens our eyes to how much the Father loves us. He touches our hardened conscience and convicts us of the guilt of our sins. He convinces us of the purity of God's holiness and the reality of his coming judgment on a wayward

> How does the Holy Spirit help us overcome our hostility toward God?

world (John 167b–8,13).[17] Finally, he assures our heart that God is trustworthy, that he is the kind of person who does what he says he is going to do. When we come to trust God's character, we can at last believe that his promise of forgiveness through Jesus is true, and not just true in general, but true for us and our sins. So the Holy Spirit inspires in us a personal faith in God so we can entrust our lives to him, his promises, and his ways.

This process of overcoming our natural resistance to God

to the point of trusting our lives to him is called conversion, a word whose root means "to turn around." When the Holy Spirit leads us through the process of conversion, we go from thinking of God as the enemy to seeing him as our rescuer. We quit running away from God and start running to him. We stop trusting only ourselves and begin at last to be able to trust the one who made us. This turn around starts in our minds, but it soon changes our hearts and then transforms our way of life.

In sport, when pro athletes are traded to the team of their old arch rivals, they have to reorient their thinking, transfer their loyalties, and change their lifestyles. The athletes they used to be in synch with are now their opponents, and their old competitors are now their teammates. The old home crowd that used to support them no longer does so, and now they are expected to play their hearts out for the crowd that used to root against them. They have to learn new plays and figure out how to get along with new players. They have to put their trust in a new coach and believe in his abilities to bring out the best in their performance. They even have to adjust their private lives by moving to a new city. Once there they may have to get involved with the local charities to support their new team's public relations efforts. They may even have to be more discreet with their night life so as to maintain their new team's good, "family" image.

In the game of life, conversion means trading sides in the conflict between the force of destruction and God's love. Before the turn around, we are on the force of destruction's team, and our acts of selfishness add to the hurt and pain of others. Afterwards, we are on God's clean-up crew. We spend our lives making this world a better place

> Do you feel like you are on a team in the game of life? What team would you like to be on?

while preparing ourselves for the next. Before the switch, we live to please ourselves. Afterwards, we are pleased to live for Christ. In conversion, the Spirit which Jesus promised to send enables people to turn to God in faith so God can turn our lives around right.

Justification

Therefore, since we have been justified through faith, we have peace with God through our Lord Jesus Christ. (Romans 5:1)

Conversion turns us to our Creator. Once we trust in Jesus, we are restored to a permanent relationship with God the Father. That's good news, because apart from knowing our Heavenly Father we don't feel whole. We can easily see how important a sense of belonging is in the world of sport. There is nothing quite like the joy of being part of a highly skilled team in perfect synch with each other as they outmaneuver their opponents. And being part of a special team makes us feel special. To find that same joy in life, God has designed human beings to need to be in synch with him as their Heavenly Father. We need to experience his fatherly love for us, if we are ever to feel that we have a worth that won't go away.

> Apart from knowing our Heavenly Father we don't feel whole.

But because our Heavenly Father is a Holy God, our sins have separated us from his presence. Our self-centeredness cuts us off from feeling like we belong to God's family. Our rebelliousness rejects any guidance from above, making us orphans who have to fend for ourselves in an often cruel and crazy world. As a result, our sin robs us of that special feeling that we are special to God, leaving us adrift in life like an athlete cut from the team.

Jesus, however, came into this world to set us free from the consequences of our sinfulness. Through his death on the cross, he opened the way for us to be cleansed from the guilt of our sins so we can be reunited with our Heavenly Father. Here's how it works. Being sinless, Jesus knows no barrier to being with God the Father. Because of his perfect holiness, Jesus has perfect access to him. Christians use a special term for having this kind of direct relationship with God. The Bible calls it having "right-standing" with God or "righteousness." Because Jesus is perfectly right with God the Father, he is able to stand in the Father's holy presence.

When we ask the Father to forgive us because of Jesus' death on our behalf, the glorious exchange takes place. Our guilt is assigned to Jesus on the cross and marked "Paid in Full." Jesus' right-standing with God is assigned to us, and we are declared "not guilty" of sin in God's eyes. The Bible uses a special word to describe sinners who have received Jesus' right-standing with God. They are said to be *justified* by God. Justification was a common legal term in Jesus' day which simply meant being declared "not guilty" in a court of law. The word even sounds like what it means: "Justified – just as if I'd never sinned."

When we are justified by God, we are acquitted on all charges of sinfulness – not only sins we have committed in the past but also those we will do in the future. Jesus' death paid for all our sins. When the justified fall short of living by agape love, they still need

Can you provide forgiveness for yourself?

to ask for forgiveness. But since God has declared them "not guilty" of all their sins because of Christ, they do not lose their right-standing with him. As a result, we can have a permanent, personal relationship with God the Father just like Jesus.

This may be a bit easier to understand if we remember that the justified are no longer orphans, but sons and daughters of God Almighty. And God responds to their disobedience like any good parent. If a teenage athlete stays out late celebrating a big victory and then comes home knocking loudly at the front door at 3:00 am what will happen? Will the parents refuse to open the door? No, of course, not. They may be really unhappy with the athlete. They may wish to discuss the matter in the morning and take some disciplinary action such as grounding their teenager for the foreseeable future. But good parents will let the offender in. Should a stranger come knock at those parents' door at 3:00 am, what will happen? They may tell him to go away. They may even call the police. But whatever they do, they won't open the door. Because of the glorious exchange made possible by the cross of Christ, those who have been justified are no longer strangers to God. They are part of his family. He may discipline them when they disobey, but he will not disown his adopted children and drive them from their new home in his presence. Through trusting in Jesus, we receive a permanent relationship with our Heavenly Father.

> When you think of God, do you feel like a stranger or a son or daughter?

Sanctification

So I say, live by the Spirit, and you will not gratify the desires of the sinful nature. The fruit of the Spirit is love, joy, peace, patience, kindness, goodness, faithfulness, gentleness and self-control. Since we live by the Spirit, let us keep in step with the Spirit. (Galatians 5:16, 22-23a, 25)

Once faith in Jesus has restored our relationship with God the Father, God the Holy Spirit makes our heart his home. In sport, teams wear the same uniform and share the same locker room, but what seals the bond among the athletes is sharing a real team spirit. In life, when we join God's team, he seals the bond between him and us by giving us the Holy Spirit. And unlike the shared spirit of a sports team, the Holy Spirit is more than just a feeling. The Holy Spirit is actually the presence of God Almighty inside of us. That makes God closer to us than even our own shadow. Because God himself lives inside us, we know that we are no longer orphans. The Spirit's presence within us is our God-given internal guarantee that makes us aware that he is our Father and we are his children. In quiet moments, the Holy Spirit enables us to have an inner sense that we are part of God's family (Romans 8:15b–16).[18]

As children often grow up to resemble their parents, the presence of the Holy Spirit in us gives us the power to grow more like our Heavenly Father. This process of becoming less selfish and more loving like God is called sanctification, a word meaning "to make holy." Here's how it works. Even after our sins are forgiven because of Jesus' death on the cross, we still have an imperfect nature that will continue to honor and serve ourselves more than God and other people. In addition to the gift of faith and the forgiveness of past sins, we need a new ability to resist sin in the future. But this ability cannot come from us as we are, since we are born with the result of Adam and Eve's disobedience. We need a new nature freed from the liabilities we have inherited from humankind's first couple. The Bible tells us that this is the work of God the Holy Spirit within us. He gives us a new nature and empowers us to fight sin.

Scripture describes the transition from the nature we are born with to the new nature given to us by the Spirit as a heart transplant: "I will give you a new heart and put a new spirit in you; I will remove from you your heart of stone and give you a heart of flesh. And I will put my Spirit in you and move you to follow my decrees and be careful to keep my laws" (Ezekiel 36:26–27). Since the old nature instinctively wanted to put ourselves first, it could not keep God's laws. But God has promised that the Spirit works to give us a new nature which wants to do our Maker's will. Whereas our old imperfect, self-centered heart was spiritually stone-cold dead, our new, agape-love-centered heart is alive and pumping spiritual nourishment into every area of our lives.

How would you describe the work of the Holy Spirit?

As a result, this transplant is like going from death to life. Our life under the power of sin kept us dead in our misdeeds, but our relationship with Christ makes us alive (Ephesians 2:1–5). When we trust in Jesus, we share in his transition from crucifixion to resurrection. When the minister puts us under the water during baptism, we are symbolically putting to death our old way of sinful living. When we are raised up from the waters, the same Spirit that raised Christ from the dead gives us the power to lead a new life under his guidance (Romans 6:1–7). That's why becoming a Christian is often called becoming "born-again." The coming of the Holy Spirit into our hearts give us a new life as if we had been born a second time with a better nature than the one we inherited from Adam and Eve (John 3:3–8).

Have you had an experience that you would attribute to the work of the Holy Spirit?

This new life necessarily gives birth to a new lifestyle. Naturally, the newly born of the Spirit have a new heart with new desires. For God himself has filled their hearts with his very own agape love through the inner presence of the Holy Spirit (Romans 5:5). Now that the Father has made them his children, they want to express their new love for him by living the way that would please God. One famous passage from the Bible contrasts the difference between our old way of living and the new:

> *The acts of the sinful nature are obvious: sexual immorality, impurity and debauchery; idolatry and witchcraft; hatred, discord, jealousy, fits of rage, selfish ambition, dissensions, factions and envy; drunkenness, orgies and the like. I warn you, as I did before, that those who live like this will not inherit the kingdom of God. But the fruit of the Spirit is love, joy, peace, patience, kindness, goodness, faithfulness, gentleness and self-control . . . Those who belong to Christ Jesus have crucified the sinful nature with its passions and desires. (Galatians 5:19-24)*

The power of the Spirit at work in us ensures that we act like people who have switched sides in the game of life. Our growing new character and conduct begin to restore us to what God had originally created us to be. As a result, the life-long process of sanctification gradually prepares us to fit in our future home in God's

> Would you like to be on the same team as those whom Jesus has restored to God and to their true selves?

eternal presence. When we finally stand face to face with our Heavenly Father, he will then at last complete the process, making us as perfect as he himself is.

Have you ever had an experience in sport that paralleled the concept of agape love?

Summary

It's one thing to watch a dramatic comeback. It's another thing completely to be part of the team on the field that's taking part in the battle. The risen Lord Jesus offers you an opportunity to be a member of his team. He will send the Holy Spirit to turn you back to trusting God. He will secure your place in God's family by extending to you his right standing with the Father. Finally, he will share with you the power of his resurrection so you can grow more in agape love every day. Through conversion, justification, and sanctification, you can get to play your part in reversing the tide of sin that seems to be winning in the world right now.

And unlike much of modern sport, in the game of life there are no spectators. Either you are on the force of destruction's team, or you have a relationship with the living Christ which puts you on God's team. Either your self-centeredness adds to the wrongs of this world. Or God the Holy Spirit works through you to be a part of the solution to the suffering and sorrow in this life. Although Christ's team may seem far behind right now, their eventual victory is a sure thing. For God has already demonstrated his power to destroy destruction by raising Jesus Christ from the dead. All that remains to be seen is who will share the incredible closeness and joy that comes from being part of Jesus' team as they work together to pull out the greatest victory the world will ever know. Jesus' team will destroy destruction forever and bring in a new and better world governed by agape love and perfect peace. The Holy Spirit is recruiting new athletes

Is the idea of switching to God's team attractive to you?

every day. He is looking to sign-up those willing to switch sides. What is your answer to him?

THE ROAD TO
JOY

CHAPTER 6

Wounds from a friend
can be trusted,
but an enemy
multiplies kisses.

Proverbs 27:6

What does it take to be a Christian athlete? Extra-ordinary goodness? No, just old-fashioned honesty. All athletes have struggles in their private lives. But sportspeople know that if you dwell too much on personal problems, you'll just get depressed and lose your mental edge. Early on in your sporting career, you learn to block out negative feelings that get you down. And you focus all your thoughts on how good you feel when you do well in sport. That's one of the great things about training. You can put out of your mind all your personal problems for hours at a time and concentrate on what you do well. So when Christians talk about human nature being infected with sin, it can easily seem like they're just trying to bring you down.

But no matter how much you ignore them, personal problems don't go away. They just go underground. They're always there in the back of your mind. They interfere with your ability to concentrate. They frustrate your friendships. They force you to put all your identity into winning. And the more you feel the pressure to win, the harder it is to perform at your best. Eventually, the longer you ignore your personal problems, the bigger the explosion will be when circumstances suddenly set them off, often for all the world to see.

At first, the claims of Christianity can seem threatening. That's because Jesus requires you to take a hard look at the very issues you are often trying very hard not to think about. It's difficult enough to admit what a constant struggle it is to win approval – whether of your father, or your coach, or your peers, or the crowd, or someone special, or yourself, or all of the above. Who wants to think about how many selfish things he has done in life as well? What could be more depressing? Only one thing – never trying to find the better way! Although painful, Christian athletes have realized that confronting the truths about themselves is the only road to finding real joy.

When high school athletes are deciding which college team to play for, they don't make their decision all at once. They go through several careful steps. First, they take a good look at themselves to try to figure out what it is they want in life. Second, they listen to the coaches to see which one really seems to understand them. Third, the athletes try to decide which

> **What decision process did you go through to choose your sport, your team?**

coaching staff will be the best at teaching them how to reach their full potential in sport. Fourth, when they have collected all the relevant information, the recruits turn to their parents and current coaches to get some solid guidance. Finally, after much thought and care, the athletes make a leap of faith. They can't be sure how everything will work out in the future. All they can do is look at the information they have right now and

choose the team that seems to be the best. Trusting they have made the right decision, the athletes sign their name to the contract and seal the deal.

Deciding to become part of God's team requires a similar careful process. First, you need to take an honest look at your life to see if where you're headed is where you want to end up. Second, you need to listen to God. Let him show you how well he knows you. Third, you need to learn from God how to fulfill your

Have you ever felt that you were trapped on the wrong team?

human potential. Let him tell you what he wants to do for you. Fourth, you need to lean on his help to make the right choice about whether to follow him. Finally, after looking at all the information, you need to decide. You can't sit on the fence. You have to leap one way or another. If you decide to become a Christian athlete, you trust your life to God and seal the deal with a prayer.

Let's go over each step.

Look

Step One: You first need to take an honest look at your life to see if where you're headed is where you want to end up.

One of the harsh realities of sport is that some people have much more natural talent than others. The less gifted can train as hard, and often much harder, and still never be as good as the gifted. It is true that natural talent alone will not carry you to the top of your sport. That takes discipline and dedication. But discipline and dedication alone rarely make up for a lack of natural ability. And just because people are talented in one sport or even one area of a given sport doesn't mean that they are necessarily as good at another. Part of being a competitive sportsperson is learning to make the most of your strengths and to be honest about your limitations.

This is true of life as well. While we naturally like to look at our strengths as people, we also need to face our limitations. And the harsh reality of life is that, because of Adam and Eve, we are born imperfect people. We may admire the life and teachings of Jesus, but none of us has the ability always to do what he says. Jesus lived a life of perfect love and encouraged humanity to do the same: "You have heard that it was said, 'Love your neighbor and hate your enemy.' But I tell you: Love your enemies and pray for those who persecute you, that you may be sons of your Father in heaven. Be perfect, therefore, as your heavenly Father is perfect" (Matthew 5:43–45a, 48). And Jesus was as good as his word. On the cross, he forgave those who crucified him. But as for us, if we're honest, we know we're different. We have enough trouble consistently loving those who love us, let alone loving those who hate us. No matter how hard we try, we can never fully live up to Jesus' teaching. In the end, our self-centeredness gets the better of us. Like the less gifted athlete, we just don't have it in us to live right as much as we would like.

Many sportspeople think if you're strong enough, you don't need God. But nothing could be further from the truth. No human being has the power to live right in his or her own strength. And we pay a high price for our

failure. We cut ourselves off from God. We condemn ourselves to the tread mill of trying to earn self-respect. We damage our relationships with others in pursuit of getting our personal needs met. And we set ourselves up for disappointment in life by expecting people and projects to satisfy our need for God. On the Day of Judgment our disappointment will turn to despair when we are sentenced to eternal death. Our self-centeredness takes us down the wrong path. We need a savior who will put us on the road to eternal life.

Christian athletes aren't weaklings grabbing for a crutch. They're the strong ones, the ones strong enough to face their lives honestly and do something about it. Some athletes come to realize they need Jesus by going through difficult circumstances. When their dreams don't come true, they see how foolish they have been to pin all their hopes for happiness on something besides God. Other athletes decide to become Christians because they have achieved their dreams. They finally reach the very top and discover it's not enough. Still feeling restless, they come face to face with how empty they are without God. Many athletes, however, manage to get just enough success to keep them looking for more. They go through life always hoping that if they can just get a little more of what they're working towards

> Do you know any athletes that keep pushing from one level of accomplishment to another in order to find satisfaction with life? Are you like this?

– a bigger victory, a nicer car, a better house, a higher salary, you name it – then they'll be happy. Athletes like these come to know Christ when they grow tired of always having to shoot for another goal because the joy of their last accomplishment was so short-lived. Christianity isn't grabbing for a crutch. It's at last being strong enough not to live a lie.

Listen

Step Two: You need to listen to God. Let him show you how well he knows you.

For many people, Christianity's claim to put people in touch with God is the very reason they decide to reject it. As far as these people are concerned, they tried God once and nothing happened. Since he didn't do what they wanted, they decided that he obviously doesn't exist. Perhaps you have had a similar experience. When you were having a really rough time, you called out to God. But nothing seemed to happen. So you gave up trying to reach God and decided to find some way to get on in life without him. The truth is, an experience like that doesn't disprove the existence of the God of the Bible. It just proves what Scripture says about the right way to approach God. If we come to God asking for what we want without first listening to what he wants, God won't hear us.

Suppose some high school runners come up to a new coach and say, "We keep losing to our opponents, give us a work-out program to increase our strength." After observing them in action, the coach realizes that their problem isn't power, but technique. Since they don't know how to put the energy their muscles produce to its best use, giving them more strength won't necessarily translate into faster times. So the coach decides not to assign them a muscle-building training schedule. He tells them that first they're going to work on how they move, before they try to put more power in their movements. The runners are stunned. They think there's nothing wrong with their technique. What they want is more

> Do you honestly recognize your strengths and weaknesses? What would your friends say about this?

power. As far as they are concerned, the coach is useless. He hasn't listened to them at all. How short-sighted of the high school runners! Instead of trusting the wisdom of their coach, they can't see beyond their own limited experience. It is easy to see that they won't get very far in sport until they learn to listen.

In life, many people call out to God when they have a problem that they want to get rid of. And God responds by going to the source. He points out their sins because he knows that their slavery to the force of destruction is the root of their struggles. He wants them to confront their sins so he can set them free. As soon as they ask forgiveness, he will rescue them from the power of destruction and give them a secure place in his family. They, however, are too busy telling God what they want to listen to God tell them what he knows they need. God wants to go to the source of their problem. They only want him to treat their symptoms. They want him to change their circumstances to their liking. God wants to change them to his liking. In the end, like those high school runners, their prayers don't get very far (Isaiah 59:1–2).[19] As a result, they become convinced that God never heard their prayer in the first place. If the only reason we try to contact God is to get him to fulfill our agenda, we will miss out on his much better agenda for us.

Have you ever felt that God didn't answer you?

If you have turned to God in the past, but haven't heard him reply, perhaps it's because you haven't been listening to what he had to say about you. Now is the time! Here are the top ten questions competitive athletes should ask God to show them about themselves:

Top Ten Questions for Athletes

10 How much do I depend on sport to make myself feel good about myself?

9 Does it give me lasting satisfaction?

8 How would I handle it if I got injured tomorrow and had to give up sport?

7 What have I had to sacrifice for sport?

6 How many friends do I now have who I feel really understand me and who feel I really understand them? How long do I keep these friends?

5 How many times have I used my sporting success to get things that make me feel good but at someone else's expense?

4 What habits do I have that I don't like but can't seem to change? How do they affect my life and my relationships?

3 Is the Bible accurate in what it says about me and my life?

2 Do I really like myself and my life as it is right now?

1 What will I say to God when I meet him face to face?

Of the top ten questions for athletes listed, which one makes you most uncomfortable? Why?

Learn

Step Three: You need to learn from God how to fulfill your human potential. Let him tell you what he wants to do for you.

Nothing shows the mettle of athletes as much as the way they respond to their coach's correction. Because having the mental edge is such an important part of winning, it's easy to be defensive when people point out a weakness in your performance. But sportspeople cannot achieve their personal best unless they are aware of where they can improve. Those who think that they know more than their coaches get defensive, ignore their wisdom, and continue to make the same mistakes that will lead to another self-inflicted defeat in the future.

Do you get defensive when you are corrected? Do you learn from your mistakes? Why do you think this is true?

Good athletes, however, know they need their coaches' help to reach their full potential. So they listen and learn. They listen and learn even when it hurts, like after they have lost a really hard-fought game where they gave everything they had and then some and still lost. A good coach will make the team sit through a play-by-play critique of all their small errors that caused them to lose. It's painful to face your failings. But successful athletes know it's the only way to get things right the next time. They grit their teeth, confront their shortcomings and deal with them on the practice field.

Nothing shows our mettle as human beings as much as our response to the truth Jesus shows us about ourselves:

Do you think the Bible accurately shows you what's wrong with your life?

In *Christ's willingness* to die for us, we see how self-centered we are. Christ's example of putting others first just shows us how much we like to live to please ourselves.

In *his wounds*, we see our own deep desire to reject the God who made us. The cruelty of crucifixion reminds us of all the times we have angrily rebelled against a God who would tell us how to live our lives.

In *his death*, we see God's ultimate answer to self-centeredness and rebellion. He will destroy it, putting those who live that way to eternal death.

In *Christ's prayer* that God forgive those who crucified him, we learn why he died. Our sin separates us from God, but he still wants a relationship with us. So on the cross Jesus offers us the glorious exchange – he takes our sins and gives us his relationship with the Father. Only by trusting in his prayer for us can we be reunited to our Heavenly Father.

In *Christ's resurrection*, we see the power the Holy Spirit has to give us a new life. When our sins are forgiven, God's Spirit lives inside us. Only then do we receive a new ability to fight our selfishness so we can love as God loves. Only then do we find the power to develop our abilities until we are the best, the very best we can be. And since the Holy Spirit raised Jesus from the dead, we can be sure that we will have eternal life, too.

It's no fun having to face the truth about yourself. So it's easy to wonder why God doesn't just welcome you back on to his team without making you admit you're a sinner. After all, the force of destruction is always there stroking your ego, telling you that you're fine just the way you are. But no good coach would tell injured athletes they're healthy enough to play when they're not. And neither does God. He wants you to see your self-centeredness for the sickness it is, so you realize that you're not up to playing on his team in your current condition. He wants you to face your situation honestly, so you realize you need his help to do something about it. He wants you to confront your sin, so you will ask Jesus Christ to be your savior.

When you ask Jesus to come into your life, he will give you life to the full. He will pull you out of the traps the force of destruction has set for you. He will break the patterns of self-defeating behavior that prevent you from getting the most out of life. In fact, Jesus will give you everything you need to fulfill the potential which was God's gift to you in the first place.

Do you think God can make a real difference in your life?

When times are hard, Jesus will be there supporting you. He will share with you the strength that kept him going when nobody believed in him any more. When times are good, Jesus will be there congratulating you. He will share with you his joy in what you have done for him, so you will find real fulfillment in what you have accomplished. In the in-between times – when you're going through your daily routine but aren't seeing much progress – he will be there encouraging you. He will remind you that God has good things for you in the future, so you can keep a positive mental attitude now. And at all times, he will be there giving you inner peace. Because he will have put his love in your heart, you will never need to fear again that you aren't good enough.

Nothing shows our mettle as human beings as much as our response to Jesus Christ. In the end, each athlete must ask: "Will I accept the Heavenly Coach's correction and sign on to his program? Or will I ignore his wisdom and live my life as I see fit – even if it's a dead-end of self-defeat? In life, will I learn or will I lose?"

Lean

Step Four: You need to lean on his help to make the right choice about whether to follow him.

Human beings were created by God to depend on him for life and strength. With him in your life, you have everything you need to reach your full potential as an athlete and as a person. Without him in your life, you condemn yourself always to fall short of God's standards and your own dreams. Trying to live life in your own strength makes as much sense as expecting meat or milk to stay fresh in the open air for months on end. They simply don't have the power in themselves to stay fresh forever. And neither do you apart from God. Eventually, one part of your life will turn sour. And when that happens, it will spoil for you whatever joy you have had from your accomplishments. You need to lean on God to be the best, the very best you can be.

Are you driven to prove you don't need anyone's help?

The Power to Change. Athletes can be hesitant to turn to God because they don't think that they have the will-power to change their lives the way God would want. For instance, they may want a relationship with God, but they don't think they can give up relations with the opposite sex. And, of course, they are right. Just because you know what you should do, doesn't mean you have the ability to do it. Their mistake is thinking that they must find this power within themselves before they can have a relationship with God. In reality, it's only when you have a relationship with God that you receive the power of the Holy Spirit for a new life of doing what's right. You need to lean on God before you can hope to change.

> Is it harder for a successful athlete than an average person to accept God's help?

The sad part of all of this is, if you tell yourself you can't come close to God until you've got your act together, you have doomed yourself to failure. You create a downward spiral. Since you need God's help to fight sin, the longer you stay away from him, the more you will sin, and the more you sin, the more you will feel you can't come to God right now. As long as you wait until you've cleaned up your act, you will never come to God. If, however, you add salt to meat or pasteurize milk, you increase its staying power tremendously. Once you invite Jesus into your life, the Holy Spirit will come to live in your heart, and He will give you the power you need to change the way you live.

The Power to Believe. Leaning on God is the only way to have the power to do what is right. Leaning on God is also the only way to have the power to believe what is right. Often people who are not yet Christians think that they have to find the inner will-

> What do you think it means to lean on God's power?

power to believe completely in God. If they have any doubts, then they must not have what it takes to be a Christian. That kind of thinking is wrong for two reasons.

First, faith is not based on our will-power, but God's work in us. That's why faith is not something we do, but something God gives us. Think about good coaches. Their players have faith in their coaching, not because the athletes have forced themselves to believe in them, but because the more the players have trained under these coaches, the more they have seen how good they really are. The faith that athletes have in good coaches is merely the natural result of getting to know them. It's only common sense, then, that in order to believe in God, you first have to get to know him. And since he has promised to show you who he is when you read the Bible, the best way to find faith is to read about Jesus and then talk to him in your heart.

Second, you shouldn't expect to have perfectly doubt-free faith in God from the very beginning. In any relationship it takes time to build trust and understanding. The first time you meet a new coach, you may get the sense that here is a person you can trust. But you can't be completely sure until you have spent time under that coach's supervision. Early on some doubts may arise. You might not understand why you are being asked to do certain things. You might not be able to see where the program is headed. But the longer you train under a good coach, the more you see how things have worked out well. And that makes you feel assured that your initial judgment was right.

Where are you with God right now?

The same is true for your faith in God. It's unrealistic to think that you won't have any doubts about God when you first start meeting him. But the more you spend time with him, the more your faith in God will grow. That's why Jesus compared faith to a mustard seed (Matthew 17:20). A mustard seed is tiny, but it can grow into a plant ten feet high. Faith in God can start small. It may be nothing more than just an inner nudging as you read the Bible telling you that it's true. But the more you feed your faith by getting to know God through prayer and Bible-reading, the bigger and stronger it will become until faith will one day fill every part of your life.

That doesn't mean, however, you have to wait until your faith is ten feet tall before you can become a Christian. All you need is just enough faith to ask God to make up for what you don't have. As one man said to Jesus, "I do believe; help me overcome my unbelief!"(Mark 9:24b) Even faith the size of a mustard seed can move all the mountains separating you from God, when you lean on God do it.

In fact, you can't have "ten-feet" faith until you have become a Christian. Getting to know God is like looking at a stained-glass window. It's far easier to understand a stained-glass window when you're on the inside of the church looking out than it is being on the outside of the church looking in. In the same way, it's far easier to understand God when he is

inside you speaking to your heart than when he is outside of you knocking to get in. Once you have invited Jesus to come into your life, his presence in your heart will confirm your faith that you were right to believe in him. As he works in you to draw you closer to the Father, you will see more evidence of the difference he has made in you, and your faith will continue to grow as a result.

Is your faith small like a mustard seed? Is it growing?

If you will lean on God with the faith you do have, Jesus will come into your life and give you more and more reasons to have even greater faith in him.

Leap

The Final Step: After looking at all the information, you have to decide. You can't sit on the fence. You have to leap one way or another. If you want to become a Christian athlete, you trust your life to God and seal the deal with a prayer.

If you were to sign a contract to play sport as a professional, you would probably be promised a great deal of money. You

might even get a signing bonus worth millions of dollars. No doubt, all that money would really change the way you live your life. But before you can spend that money and enjoy all the benefits of your newfound wealth, you still must do one thing. You have to sign your name to the check and present it to the bank. You could simply put the check in your billfold. The millions would still be set aside for you, but you wouldn't be able to enjoy any of the benefits until you presented the check to the bank. If you waited to cash the check long enough, one day the check would no longer be any good. And you would have missed your opportunity to change your life.

Now, only the very top athletes receive a check for millions of dollars as a signing bonus. But because of Jesus' death on the cross, God offers to give you and everyone else something far more valuable for changing your lives. He offers to write you a check which entitles you to deposit Jesus' right-standing with God in your heavenly account. Will you cash the check?

In the end, you must look at all the information and decide one all-important question: Who is Jesus? He claimed to be the Son of God who could forgive sin and conquer death. Is he a liar? Is he a lunatic? Or is he who he said he is, the Savior and Lord of humankind.[20] If Jesus is the great moral teacher everyone says he is, his words must be trustworthy. And if he says that he is the way to God the Father, then it is only reasonable to take him at his word and entrust your life to him. The decision to believe in God and commit yourself to serve him is not a leap into the dark. It's a leap into the clear light of Jesus' trustworthiness.

> Have you seriously considered accepting God's forgiveness? Does his rescue plan make sense to you?

If you want to become a Christian athlete, here's your chance to cash the check God has written in your name. If you want to sign on to God's team, seal the deal with the following prayer.

Heavenly Father,

I trust you. Thank you for loving me despite the many times I have disappointed you.

I confess that I have rebelled against your authority and made up my own rules to suit myself.

As a result, I have offended you, hurt other people and let myself down. Remembering my sins fills me with regret, but I am powerless to change my situation.

I am now not fit to be part of your eternal family. But in your great love for me, you sent your Son Jesus Christ to take my punishment in my place so that I can share his right-standing with you instead.

For Jesus' sake, please forgive me all that is past. For his sake, please fill me full of your Holy Spirit now and in the future. From this day forward, give me the power to lead a new life as a member of your family, following you in your service and loving you and all you have made.

I ask this because I love you and want Jesus Christ to be my personal Savior and Lord now and forever.

Thank you for hearing me and sending him into my life, for it is through him that I have prayed. Amen.

Did you say the suggested prayer? Whom should you tell to share the joy?

Love

If you prayed this prayer, you are now a Christian. Jesus has come into your life, and the Holy Spirit has come into your heart. From now on, you have a personal relationship with God. And that will make all the difference as you go through life. Remember the three childhood joys of sport – release, relationships, and a reputation? In each of these areas Jesus will give you more fulfillment than you have ever had before, even more than sport. And the more you experience the joy he gives, the more you will love him. That's because you will now know for yourself:

Jesus is the better way.

Do you feel different after accepting God's forgiveness? Do strong feelings make it more true? Remember that we are to walk by faith and not by our feelings.

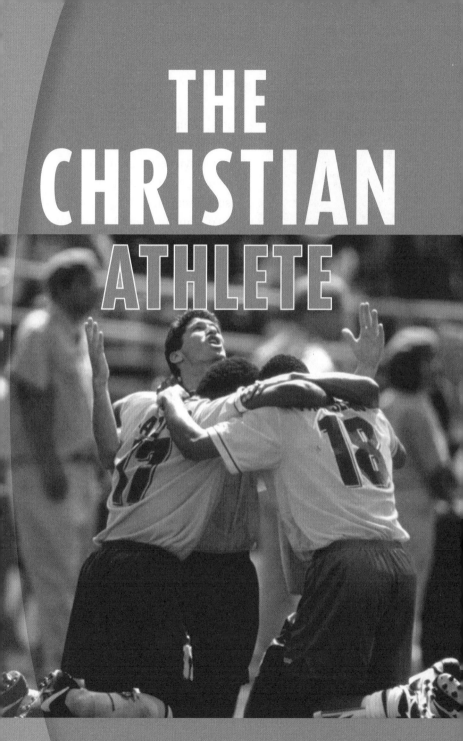

THE
CHRISTIAN
ATHLETE

Christian sportspeople often make a point of acknowledging God's help in their athletic performance. It is common today in interviews after a game to hear a player start off by saying something like, "First of all, I just want to give all the glory to my Lord Jesus Christ." Talk like that sometimes makes other people think that the only reason these athletes became Christians was so they could get supernatural help in winning. But that isn't it at all! In honest humility, Christian sportspeople recognize that the only reason they have any talent in the first place is that it's God's gift. And they want others to know that they appreciate God helping them to develop it to their maximum athletic potential. Still, their maximum potential can easily be less than a non-Christian's. After all, the Bible says that God is so loving he gives his good gifts to all, to those who love him and acknowledge his gift and to those who don't know him and take all the credit for themselves (Matthew

You will show me
the path of life;
in your presence
is the fullness of joy,
at your right hand
are pleasures
for evermore.

Psalm 16:11[21]

5:45). So being a Christian athlete isn't a surefire way to become an athletic champion!

But winning in sport isn't the reason someone becomes a Christian. Winning in life is! As has been discussed earlier,

Do you expect God to help you win? Or are you ultimately searching for real relationships and real joy?

the thrill of victory doesn't last long, even for a Christian. If all God meant to Christian athletes was as a crutch to help them perform better, then Christian champions would be just as empty on the inside as non-Christians! Sport, no matter how good you are at it, can't solve your problems in life. And you only set yourself up for major disappointment when you pour your heart and soul into winning thinking that it can. No, Christian sportspeople look to God for something far more important than just as an insurance policy for winning. They look to God to give them at long last the deep fulfillment they have always been searching for. In Jesus they find real joy, because he gives them real release, real relationships, and a reputation for being REAL.

Real Release

Sport provides a way to escape from the pressures of life, *for a while*. But time spent doing sport does nothing to help solve the problems that cause the pressures in the first place. So sport can end up being a way of running from yourself and your life. And that will only add to your difficulties. Time spent with God is different. He's the better way to find release because God actually helps you deal with the sources that are causing your problems. God shows you the truth about yourself and your life.

> Do you use sport to escape from your problems?

Here are the two biggest sources of stress in life:
1. Being frustrated that you aren't in control of your circumstances.
2. Being fearful that you aren't good enough as you are.

When you think about it, most problems in life boil down to one or the other, or both. Angry about being injured? That's being frustrated that you aren't in control of your circumstances. Feeling rejected because of a relationship gone sour? That's being fearful that you aren't good enough as you are. Devastated by a loss in which you gave everything you had? That's both being frustrated that you aren't in control of your circumstances and being fearful that you aren't good enough as you are. Sport isn't much help in solving problems like these. But God is.

> What were some times when you weren't in control? When were you frustrated because you feared you weren't good enough?

Being frustrated that you aren't in control. From the very beginning the force of destruction has tried to get humankind to believe a fundamental lie: "If you try hard enough, you can determine your own destiny." That's the lie of self-aggrandizement, i.e., claiming to have more power in life than you really do. The honest truth is no one can control all the circumstances of his or her life. And when events spin out of your control, you are forced to face your powerlessness to make things any better. No wonder you end up feeling frustrated!

But God is pure power working in pure love. He *is* in charge of all things. And he has promised to work together for good all things that happen in the lives of his children, both good and bad (Romans 8:28). You may not have the power to bring good out of the bad in your life, but God does and *will*. Just as he raised Christ from the dead, he will bring you joy even out of seemingly hopeless situations. When you are frustrated by your circumstances, spending time with God can give you peace of mind. That's because being with God reminds you to trust his love for you, since you can count on him to do good for you.

Being fearful that you aren't good enough. From the very beginning, the force of destruction has tried to get

> Have you seen God work things out when you stopped controlling the situation? Have you seen God make a bad thing turn out as a good thing?

humankind to believe a second fundamental lie: "You have to prove your self-worth." That's the lie of self-doubt, i.e., you have to doubt your self-worth unless you can show concrete evidence to the contrary. The honest truth is that you can't do anything to prove your own worth because only being loved by God gives you a sense of worth that won't go away. So the more you strain to show how important you are, the more you become a slave to always having to show how important you are. No wonder you end up fearful that you don't have enough self-worth!

Could you feel important without winning or without your sport?

But God is pure love acting with pure power. Your Heavenly Father has lavished his agape love on you because you are his child (1 John 3:1). And he has promised that nothing can separate you from this love which you have received because of Jesus (Romans 8:38–39). God has declared you good enough in Christ – who can contradict God Almighty? Not any circumstance, not any detractor, not any lie of the force of destruction. The cross testifies for all time to the unconditional, unchanging worth you have in God's eyes. You are forever precious in his sight! When you're anxious because you doubt yourself, spending time with God can give you peace of mind. Because when you are with God, the power of his love will break through the lies of the enemy to remind you to trust your true value in Christ.

The Bible. Experiencing the peace of God brings the best release and relaxation that is possible in this life. So how do you spend time with him so you can get it? Since peace of mind comes from trusting God's promises to you, it's only common sense that you should begin by reading God's book of promises, the Bible! The more you regularly read the Bible the better you will know God and the less you will believe the enemy's lies which seek to steal your peace. But you need to do more than just read about what God has promised to do for you. You need to *act* to show you really believe them. The more you express your trust in the Bible's promises, the more you honor God. And the more you honor God, the easier it will be to sense God's presence with you and the more you will drive your enemy far away from you. Christians normally express their faith in God's promises in three ways: praise, prayer, and thanksgiving.

Praise. The first way of expressing your trust in God is

> Peace of mind comes from trusting God's promises to you.

to let him know that you think he's great because of who he is and what he has promised to do for you. Telling God how much you admire him is called giving him praise. And when we praise God, we give him the honor which Adam and Eve failed to do when they were tempted. So expressing our faith through praise actually begins to reverse the work of sin in this world. What was the first consequence of Adam and Eve's disobedience? They hid from God. If praise reverses the enemy's work, it's only logical, then, that praising God permits us to begin to re-enter his presence. And so the Bible tells us that we should approach God through praise.

One of the best ways to express praise is by singing songs. From the beginning of human history, when people fall in love, they sing songs to each other to say how wonderful the

> "Enter his gates with thanksgiving and his courts with praise; give thanks to him and praise his name." (Psalm 100:4)

other person is for making their own life so much better. It's no different with us and God. The Bible tells us that we should come before God's presence with singing (Psalm 100:2). In fact, a whole book of the Bible is devoted to songs to be sung to God. It's called the Book of Psalms, and these ancient songs praise God for the wonders of his creation, for his consistent love, and for his faithfulness in keeping all his promises. And there's no better reason to praise God than for being so loving as to give you a worth that won't go away through Jesus Christ. That's why for almost two thousand years, every generation of Christians have written their own songs of praise for Jesus, the best of which has been gathered together in church hymnals and songbooks for our use today.

When we sing God's praises, we leave behind the worries of this life and focus on God's presence with us and the peace that he brings to our lives. That's why church services usually

begin with singing. In fact, many informal Christian churches begin their Sunday service with 20- to 30-minutes of songs. That's so people can concentrate on experiencing the peace that comes from expressing their faith in God through praise.

Prayer. Second, you can show you trust that God cares for you by taking all your cares and concerns to God in prayer. Prayer is simply taking the time to talk to God as you would any other person. You share what's going on in your

> "Cast all your anxiety on him because he cares for you." (1 Peter 5:7)

life with him, telling him what's happening and asking his help with difficult situations. You should also bring to him the problems of other people you care about and want him to help. And you should always spend some time listening for what he wants to say to you about anything you've mentioned or some other topic that he wants to bring up. Like any conversation, prayer needs to be a two-way activity.

When you pray, it's always good to include references to God's promises as part of the conversation. For instance, say you are injured and you miss a really important competition as a result. Naturally, you raise the issue with God because it's probably the most important thing happening in your life right now. You tell him your frustrations about what has happened. You can even tell him if you are angry with him because of the way things have worked out so far. But you finish off by reminding him (and yourself!) of his promise to work everything to good for those who love him and ask him to do just that in this situation. Having unburdened your problems to God and remembered his promises to do something about them, your time in prayer will leave your heart lighter and your mind at peace.

Thanksgiving. The third, and most difficult, way to express your trust in God is to thank him for being trustworthy, even when things aren't going the way you would like. Overflowing thankfulness in all situations is the hallmark of the mature Christian. With all the ups and downs of competitive life, it's hard not to get discouraged sometimes. But Christians show their trust in their Heavenly Father when they can look disappointment in the eye and thank God. They know that their value in Christ remains the same and that their Heavenly Father will work this event for good in some area of their life. That kind of faith in God doesn't come all at once. But as you learn to thank God regardless of your situation, you experience a deeper release than you will have ever known before. The Bible calls this release the peace that passes all understanding.

> "So then, just as you received Christ Jesus as Lord, continue to live in him, rooted and built up in him, strengthened in the faith as you were taught, and overflowing with thankfulness." (Colossians 2:6-7)

Why? Because there's no earthly reason why you should be able to be at peace in such circumstances. But isn't that just when you really need a surefire release from stress? God will give you this special peace when you express your trust in him through thanksgiving.

> "Do not be anxious about anythng, by prayer and petition, with thanksgiving, present your requests to God. And the peace of God, which transcends all understanding, will guard your hearts and your minds in Christ Jesus." (Philippians 4:6-7)

Quiet Time. Because Bible-reading, prayer, praise, and thanksgiving are so important to your relationship with God, committed Christians are encouraged to have a daily "spiritual work-out" called a quiet time. Every individual develops a

pattern for interacting with God which fits his or her own personality and maturity in Christ. Still, a common outline goes something like this:

■ Consistency. You make a regular appointment with God, either before your day begins or before you go to bed, for a set period of time. Many beginners start by setting aside fifteen minutes.

When are you at your best for a quiet time? Are you sharper in the morning or at night?

■ Praise. You open your time with God by praising him, either through reading some psalms or singing a couple of Christian songs. Use this time of praise to leave behind all the concerns weighing on your mind and concentrate instead on the wonders of God's character.

■ Bible-reading. Then you read a passage from the Bible and think about what it is saying. Remember, the whole point of reading the Bible is so you can grow closer to God by learning to trust him to draw you ever closer to himself. So ask yourself three questions: What does this passage tell me about who God is and what his character is like? What does this passage tell me about what God has promised to do for me? And what help does this passage tell me I need to ask from God so I can respond to him as I should? There are several different daily Bible-reading plans with notes on the passages to help you. You can find a selection of them in any Christian bookstore.

■ Prayer. Now you bring your concerns to God. You begin by asking his forgiveness for shortcomings you have on your conscience or those brought to mind by the biblical passage. This is called confession. Next, you remember to God the difficult situations your friends are going through. This is called intercession. Finally, you discuss your own life with him. You remember the Bible-reading and ask him to make you more like what you read. You then present to him the problems you are facing right now. These are called petitions. At each stage of prayer you always pause to listen to God's response which will help guide you in what to pray next.

■ Thanksgiving. After unburdening your heart, you thank God for all that he has done, including forgiving your sins and hearing your prayers.

How much you get out of your quiet time depends on your approach. Unlike athletic training, you can't make yourself grow spiritually by sheer force of will power and hard work.

This fundamental principle is true, even when what you're doing is something as spiritual as reading the Bible and praying. Stop and think about it. You didn't rescue yourself from sin. You can't fight sin and do right on your own, either. Our natural tendency as human beings is to try to do things *for* God in our own strength. But God wants us to do all things *through* him in his power. Always remember, holiness is the result of ever-increasing dependence on God. If you want your quiet time to be regular and refreshing, you need to look to God and lean on his promises to make this happen. As you do, you will develop an intimate relationship with God. And to know God is to know real release because of his special peace.

Real Relationships

Having a meaningful relationship with God opens the door for you to have lots of meaningful relationships with other people, too. With God as your Heavenly Father, you now have a welcome place in his large, extended family that's called the church. So Christians are even closer than teammates. They're family! No Christian should be a "born-again orphan," trying to follow God on his or her own. That makes as much sense as expecting newborn babies to survive on the street by themselves. Since you are a part of Christ's family, you never need to feel alone again.

> Do you find that athletes tend to stand apart from others?

Like any family, the church has people of all different ages, experiences, and personalities. Naturally, you will feel closer to some members of the family than others. And, of course, they're all human, so they will make mistakes. It doesn't take long to learn that the church on earth isn't perfect. But, despite their shortcomings, these are the people God has promised to live among. They share a common experience of having their lives turned around by his agape love, and they share a common commitment to show that love to other people. Because he cares for you, God has provided a loving, earthly family to give you the concrete help you need to make your life the best, the very best it can be.

Acceptance. It has been said that home is the place where, when you go there, they have to let you in. In spite of all its imperfections, the church is the place you can call home. Why? Because the church family is the one place on earth where people are committed to accepting you as good enough because of what Christ has done for you. With Jesus as your Savior and Lord, you are a member of his family. And the church is called to welcome you as you are, with all your good points and all your bad points. While church members cannot approve of any sins you may commit, they are committed to helping you struggle to overcome them. They will always love you, even when

> Do you think that you are accepting of others? Would you characterize yourself as critical or judgmental?

they cannot in good conscience love your actions. They will, of course, expect you to return the favor!

That's good news, because mutual acceptance is the key

to meaningful relationships. Most of the time we never get beyond the surface with other people because we only want to let our best side show. Deep down, we're afraid others might not think much of us, if they really knew what we were like. Take a look at dating relationships. Who hasn't spent endless energy trying to hide their drawbacks and highlight their assets just so someone special might decide they were good enough to go out with. But as long as you hide what you think are your drawbacks, you will never feel free to be who you really are. And there's not much real joy in a relationship like that.

Are you able to be honest and vulnerable with others?

For any relationship to be truly meaningful, you have to be able to give all of yourself to it. And if you give your all in a relationship, you have to give both your good and your bad. They're a package deal. But the same is true for those who you are interested in. If other people give you their all, they'll give both their good and their bad. That's why real relationships need a "Safety Zone." Both parties need to feel that the other is committed to overlooking their weaknesses and encouraging their strengths. Only then will each feel safe enough to give all to the other. And the church is the best "Safety Zone" there is. Since the members know what it is to be accepted by God despite their shortcomings, they are able to do the same for others. Relationships with other Christians are real because God's acceptance of his children enables them to accept each other.

Do you enable others to disclose important things about themselves?

Understanding. Because Christians are all part of the same family, they share more than just a mutual acceptance – they share a common history which gives them a similar outlook on life. They became Christians when they asked Jesus Christ to be their Savior and Lord. That means they understand what it is to be a sinner. That means they understand what it is to try to live in keeping with the Spirit. So they understand how you see yourself, and they know firsthand the kind of struggles you now go through. As fellow Christians, they know what makes you tick because they tick the same way. Because these people have the same personal insight and experience as you do, you can share your life fully with them. And finding a friend like that is a genuine cause for joy! Relationships in the church family are real because Christians tick together.

Encouragement. Because the church family knows where you are coming from and where you want to go, they are uniquely able to help you get there.

■ *Pastors teach* you the Bible so that you can learn to hear God's voice for yourself and apply his truth to your life.

■ *Older Christians* offer you a concrete example of how to live as a child of God. And from the wealth of their experience, they can give you good advice for growing in Christ. Many Christian groups have programs where older Christians spend time studying the Bible with new Christians so they can pass on to them the important lessons they have learned in life.

■ *Members of the church family your own age* act as companions with you on the Christian journey. Peers in Christ can share all of your life as you go through each stage of life. Once you grow close to another Christian, the closeness stays, even if you no longer live near each other. Because of the special bond Christians share with each other, friendships in Christ always remain fresh. It will seem like old times every time you have an opportunity to update another on what's been happening in your life.

Some congregations try to encourage close Christian friendships among people of the same age through accountability groups. Typically, these groups consist of a small number of people (6–8) who are committed to meeting together weekly. They study the Bible, pray for one another and encourage each other to grow spiritually. Members of these groups know each other well enough to be able to help each other with those areas of their Christian life where they are the weakest.

> Do you meet regularly with a small group of Christian friends?

■ *Christian sport organizations* try to meet the specific needs and concerns of Christian athletes. They link up like-minded sportspeople so they can mutually support one another to develop athletically and spiritually. Naturally, the

older Christian athletes in these groups are invaluable for helping you keep winning and losing in a biblical perspective. Christian relationships are real because they help you get to where you really want to go.

Mission. Christians are all heading in the same direction because they all have a share in the family business – reversing the work of the force of destruction in this world. Naturally, the chief aim of their task is to help reunite human beings with their Heavenly Father through Jesus Christ. For keeping people away from God is the chief effect

What is your mission in life?

of the Enemy's handiwork. Christians carry out the family business on two levels: personal and through the local church congregation.

■ *Personal*. All Christians are called to show love for others in their every day dealings. There is no better way to make your faith look credible in the eyes of others than by demonstrating a character influenced by the Holy Spirit. One of the early tests for young Christians is how they treat their old friends who do not yet share their new faith. Many times new Christians can no longer do some of the same things they used to with their old friends. The temptation, then, is either to spend all your time together talking about your new faith when you're with your old friends or not to see them at all. Neither is really loving. Talking too much about your faith can be a real turn-off. And spending no time with your old friends will leave them feeling angry and rejected.

Do you spend time with old friends?

The Bible says you should love people enough to share not only the good news of Jesus Christ but your life as well (I Thessalonians 2:8). Often that means finding ways to spend time with your old friends doing things they enjoy, but which aren't incompatible with your own faith. With fellow athletes, doing some kind of sport together is always a good neutral activity which you both can enjoy. Remember, Christ is more often *caught* by being around the love of Christians than *taught* by incessant harping on the truths of the Bible. The more "not-yet" Christians sense you care about them, the more interested they will be in listening to you explain why they should become one.

Are you able to be with your old friends without being tempted by your old bad habits?

■ *The local church congregation*. Individual Christians are asked by their Heavenly Father to be ambassadors for his love in every aspect of their daily lives. Nevertheless, God has instituted the church family as his chief witness to his presence in this world and as his chief agent through which he likes to work. Why? A relationship with God is based on trust in his love. What better testimony to the presence of his love than the visible relationships of members of church congregations? Restoring people to relationships based on love is God's work in this world. Who better to encourage such relationships than a community of people who are already practicing what God wants them to preach? Christians as a church family have a larger impact in this world than as individuals because together they can give evidence to the transforming power of agape love relationships.

Therefore, all new Christians are expected to join a local church congregation. Here you should commit to spend "family time" every Sunday when the whole church gathers to worship God together. Here you should commit to give financially to support the congregation's ministry to its members and mission to its community. Here you should commit to give of your time and talents to the running of some aspect of this work.

Do you have a church home? If not, what can you do about it?

You might decide to help with the congregation's ministry to children and youth. Or you might volunteer to take part in its outreach to the community. Since Jesus preached salvation to sinners and sought to help the poor, we should try to do both, too. Your congregation may sponsor evangelistic events like a Christian concert to which you can bring your old friends. But it may also offer you the opportunity to help those in need by doing things like serving at a soup kitchen or volunteering at a homeless shelter. Some congregations even have special-interest groups that seek to counter the force of destruction at work in the laws and customs of our society. Groups that seek to protect the sanctity of life, promote racial reconciliation, fight against the exploitation of women and children through pornography, or work for more economic fairness for the poor are just some examples.

Although as an athlete your free time can be fairly limited, it is important to take part in the work of your congregation in some way. Because becoming a Christian means committing yourself to serving God through a local congregation while this world lasts.

How do you think you might want to serve through the church?

Summary. Relationships in the church family are real because they're well-rounded. They're based on mutual acceptance and understanding. They're expressed through mutual encouragement and a common mission. Christian relationships bring joy easily, because they have something as powerful as Jesus at their root. And since they are grounded in Christ, like his love, Christian relationships will last for ever. You can't get more real than that.

A Reputation for Being REAL

As soon as you become a Christian, you will get a new reputation. It won't take long for your fellow athletes to project on to you their own feelings about the Almighty. If they basically respect the idea of God, they will show you respect as the "spiritual" one. If they're running away from God, they'll try to keep you far away by putting you down as the "religious fanatic." There's not a whole lot you can do to change their initial reaction to your new faith. But as time goes on and you grow in Christ, whether other athletes consider you "spiritual" or a "fanatic," they will come to learn that you are also strong,

wise, loving and, of all the people they know, the most fully alive. In other words, the longer your life is shaped by Christ's love, the more you will develop a reputation for being REAL.

Strong. Although those who make fun of you will never tell you, the longer you take their comments in stride, the more

> As soon as you become a Christian, you will get a new reputation.

they will come to respect you for being able to be your own person. And the longer you continue to train hard and show your firm commitment to athletic excellence, the more they will come to admit that becoming a Christian doesn't mean that you lose your drive to be the best. In fact, your faith will enable you to train even more consistently. Because of the peace in your life, you will be able to work just as hard during the times you see no progress as those when you do. Your strength as a Christian will give you strength as an athlete. And those around you will eventually make the connection.

> Do you find that people accept you for what you do or who you are?

Wise. As your fellow athletes come to admire your strength in the Spirit and in sport, they will come to respect the insight into life that special combination gives you. After all, you have taken a hard look at yourself and the athletic journey. You have faced the very things that are causing them problems but which they have chosen to ignore. Because you aren't on the treadmill of earning self-worth, you can see what's going on in their life better than they can. Because you understand human nature, you can see the self-defeating habits in their life which they're blind to. If you dispense your comments sparingly, on invitation and in a low-key, non-threatening manner, your fellow athletes will learn to listen. And as they hear your wisdom, they will see you really do know how to be a winner in life.

> Do you tend to be gentle and caring when you give advice or are you discouraging and biting?

Loving. But even more than your words of wisdom, your small, daily acts of concern for others will set you apart from your peers. In the world of sport, looking out for number one is always priority number one. If you can attend to your own sporting priorities *and* find the energy to encourage others in theirs, you will shine out brighter than an Olympic gold medal. If you don't regularly work hard on your own athletic development, sportspeople won't respect you. But, if you don't regularly work hard at supporting others, sportspeople will write off your faith as just another trendy technique for self-improvement through mental training. If, however, you can regularly make other athletes feel important, not because of their performance in sport, nor even because of their willingness to listen to things of the Spirit, but solely because of God's love for them, then your works will match your words. And people will see that it's God who is working in their lives through your love.

Alive. As you grow in Christ, you will come to an ever-increasing appreciation that your strength, wisdom, and love are not products of your sweat for God, but the work of God's Spirit in you. Otherwise, your faith would be just another exercise in you trying to earn approval. And the strivings of self always end in disappointment, even if they have a religious packaging. But the things of the Spirit are different. The Spirit gives birth to life in all its fullness. After all, God gave Adam the gift of life when he breathed his own Spirit into the earthen form he had modeled out of the dust.

> "The LORD God formed the man from the dust of the ground and breathed into his nostrils the breath of life, and the man became a living being." (Genesis 2:7)

Although Adam and Eve lost that indwelling presence of God, because of Christ, the Holy Spirit is once again in your heart. The more you actively lean on God and hold on to his promises, the more the Spirit will be at work in you to bring every area of your being under his rule. And the stronger the presence of the Holy Spirit is in your life, the more you will know firsthand the fullness of joy that his presence brings. For wherever the Spirit rules, there is forever freedom from the treadmill of earning self-worth. Wherever the Spirit rules, there is God's agape love forever assuring you of your eternal worth in his eyes. What greater causes for joy could there be in this life? So the more you are filled with God's Spirit, the more you will be made fully alive with living joy. And when that happens, even your detractors will realize that God's love has made you REAL, now and forever.

> "When a man's ways are pleasing to the LORD, he makes even his enemies live at peace with him." (Proverbs 16:7)

Don Lash

Can Christian faith and competitive sport really be compatible? According to this book, Jesus Christ gives the real release, relationships, and reputation that alone satisfy the longing of your heart. As a result, faith in Christ acts as the only fireplace strong enough for your competitive desire to burn safely. Well, that's the argument of *Real Joy*. But you may ask, will it really work in the tough world of top competitive sport? Can a champion athlete be both loving of others and determined to win? Consider the incredible story of Don Lash.

On June 13, 1936, Don Lash of Indiana did the unthinkable. He broke the world record that everyone thought was unbeatable, the two-mile time set by Paavo Nurmi of Finland five years previous. On July 3, 1936, Don Lash did the exceptional. He set a new American record in the 10,000 meters, finishing 140 yards ahead of the next competitor, and qualifying for the 1936 Olympics. But on July 12, 1936, Don Lash did the inconceivable. In the new Randall's Island, New York, stadium, he was competing in the final Olympic Trials for the 5,000 meters, the Olympic event closest to his world record in the two-mile.

Don set a solid pace. And by the two-third's mark, he had built up a forty-yard lead. But, it was a hot day, and some of the runners were struggling. In fact, four of the twelve wouldn't be able to finish the race. So Don broke the first rule of competition. He looked back to see how the others were doing. Then he broke the second rule of competition. Don actually became concerned about one of them, his good friend and fierce competitor, Tommy Deckard. As teammates at Indiana, they pushed each other hard in practice, with Tommy often winning. When Don won his Olympic berth in the 10,000 meters, Tommy had finished fourth, just missing a spot on the team for Berlin. This race was his last chance. And Tommy was not faring very well today, either. He was at the back of the pack of those still in contention.

Then, Don didn't break another rule of competition, he broke the mold. The "Iron man from Indiana" did the inconceivable. In an Olympic Trial, in his best event, his best chance at an Olympic Medal, his best shot at fulfilling his dream and satisfying the expectations of a demanding nation, Don let four runners pass him as he dropped back to his younger teammate. He turned to his good friend and fierce competitor and said, "Come on, Tommy, you can do it. Just stay with me."[22] With three laps to go, Tommy stayed with Don, and Don stayed with Tommy. And one by one, the two of them together passed the other competitors. On the back stretch of the last lap they took the lead. But at the head of the home stretch, Louis Zamperini challenged the pair, passing them both. As the finish line approached and Tommy was assured of at least third place, qualifying him for the Olympic team, Don at last turned on his

> Did Don Lash show compassion or disregard for his sport in assisting his friend? Should this happen at such a high level of competition?

kick. He out-sprinted Zamperini, closing in at the very end. Drawing just even, Don finished in a dead heat for first by sticking out his barrel chest at the tape. As Arthur Daley of the New York Times put it, Don had won "not one place but two."[23]

Any competitor will tell you that in the heat of competition you don't have time to think and ponder, to contemplate leisurely whether you should do this or that. In competition, you can only rely on instincts built up by years of proper training. Don Lash didn't have time to think what he was doing that day at Randall's Island. He had spent years training his heart to love others while he was training his body to lead all his competitors. And in a race where everything was on the line, Don Lash was true to his training in both. He risked everything to help a friend, and fought with everything he had to finish first. Not surprisingly, Don developed a reputation for being a real champion who was also real. So much so, that in 1938 he was awarded the coveted Sullivan Award, given to the most outstanding American athlete of his time. In his citation, he was described as "unselfish and self-sacrificing for the good of his teammates" with that day on Randall's Island specifically mentioned.[24] Winner of twelve national long-distance running titles, Don Lash was recognized as a fierce competitor. He was respected even more for his unfailing love.[25]

Can you imagine another Don Lash in today's sporting climate?

To make a permanent difference for Christ in the world of sport, Don became one of the early leaders of the Fellowship of Christian Athletes. It was his great dream that generations of athletes would come to know the love of Jesus Christ so that they, too, could become real champions who were REAL.[26]

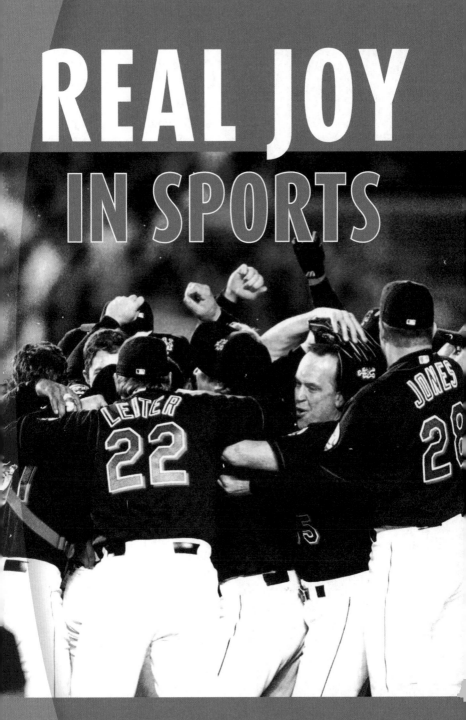

REAL JOY
IN SPORTS

Jesus said, "Therefore everyone who hears these words of mine and puts them into practice is like a wise man who built his house on the rock. The rain came down, the streams rose, and the winds blew and beat against that house; yet it did not fall, because it had its foundation on the rock. But everyone who hears these words of mine and does not put them into practice is like a foolish man who built his house on sand. The rain came down, the streams rose, and the winds blew and beat against that house, and it fell with a great crash."

Matthew 7:24-27

To be the best, the very best. To be on the award stand with the crowd on its feet for you. To see *your* flag raised, to hear *your* national anthem played, to feel the weight of the gold medal hanging from *your* neck – who wouldn't want to live that dream! Many athletes sacrifice everything they have to try to make that dream a reality. They give up all their outside interests. They learn to get along without many meaningful friendships. They put their whole heart and soul into pursuing victory – all because the prize seems worth the price.

But is it? Consider the film *Chariots of Fire*. Its story compares two top British sprinters at the 1924 Paris Olympics – Harold Abrahams, who ran to prove his worth, and Eric Liddell, who ran because he felt God's pleasure when he went fast.

As a Jewish student at Cambridge University in the 1920s, Harold was made to feel inferior because of his ethnic background. He ran track to prove that he was not just as good but even better than the English aristocracy that quietly snubbed him. But his sporting success was no solution. In the scene showing his pre-race rub down, Harold confides his deepest fears to Aubrey Montague, a Cambridge friend and Olympic teammate:

> Do you ever find yourself doubting that the prize is worth the price? What have you eliminated from your life for the sake of the prize?

I'm twenty-four – and I've never known [contentment]. I'm forever in pursuit – and I don't even know what it is I'm chasing. Aubrey, old chap – I'm scared . . . In one hour's time, I'll be out there again. I'll raise my eyes and look down that corridor – four feet wide with ten lonely seconds to justify my whole existence. But will I! . . . Aubrey, I've known the fear of losing . . . but now, I'm almost too frightened to win.

In this candid moment, Harold admitted the harsh reality of his situation. He was running in place on the treadmill. And no athletic victory, not matter how great, was going to enable him to get off. Contentment to be himself would not come from athletic achievement, no matter how glorious to others. And he was right. He won, the first Englishman ever to win the Olympic 100 meters. But after the race, he remained silent and withdrawn, even from his friends. In the end, he simply went out that night and got drunk with his coach.

> After training so long and only having the excitement last for a few hours, have you ever felt like saying, "Is that it?"

Eric Liddell, on the other hand, didn't expect sport to give him contentment in life. He trusted God and his promises for that. "The Flying Scotsman" ran because God had gifted him athletically. He wanted to enjoy what he had been given, and use his gift to help others come to share the joy he knew in Jesus. As a student at Edinburgh University, Eric had decided to become a missionary to China like his parents. But he felt he had a task to do at home before he could leave for that distant land. He wanted to finish developing his athletic talent, savoring to the full the joy God gave him when he pushed his body to the limit. And he also wanted to share his love of God with those in his own country who shared his love of sport. Always combining his faith and his sport, Eric looked to the Paris Olympics as the pinnacle of his athletic career.

It was devastating, then, when Eric learned that at Paris his specialty, the 100 meter race, involved running on Sunday. According to the teaching of his church in Scotland, Sunday was set aside exclusively for worshipping God. Being a man of integrity, he refused to run in that event. Since God was the source of Eric's running, winning a gold medal against God's rules would only rob God of his honor and Eric's running of its joy. In the film, he sits in the stands with friends, ready to cheer Harold to victory. When asked if he had any regrets, Eric replies, "Regrets, aye! Doubts, no!"

> Could you let go of your best event if it meant being the best man or woman of integrity?
> Which is better, winning through drugs or competing with honor?

Since Eric didn't run in the 100 meters, however, he was entered into the 400 meters as a sort of consolation prize. Now a sprinter competing in a middle-distance event at that elite level didn't have much of chance. But, at least, Eric would be able to say he had competed in the

Olympic Games. What a total surprise, then, when Eric not only did not fade as the race went on but did the opposite. He speeded up, setting a world record on his way to an Olympic gold medal. The crowd went wild. And Eric? Naturally, he was filled with joy! He had trusted God to work everything to good, and God did – in fact, far more abundantly than Eric could have asked for or imagined (Ephesians 3:20). Because Eric had had the courage to choose God over gold, God in his love had decided to give Eric both. Psalm 126 must have gone through his mind:

> *We were like men who dreamed. Our mouths were filled with laugher, our tongues with songs of joy. Then it was said among the nations, "The LORD has done great things for them." The LORD has done great things of us, and we are filled with joy. (Psalm 126:1b–3)*

Do you know someone who lives a life of real joy? Do you?

In a haunting image, the film shows Harold looking on at Eric's real joy, in amazement, in approval, in acute longing.

The Better Best

The athletic dream says that all your problems will fade away, if you can just make it to the top, the very top, of your sport. In reality, many elite athletes find themselves deeply disappointed when they get there. Unlike the vast majority of sportspeople who never make it to that level, champions learn first-hand the hard truth that superior athletic success, by itself, won't make you happy. If you are miserable on the inside before you win an Olympic gold medal, you will still be miserable afterwards. A gold medal outside doesn't change what's on the inside. Sporting success cannot solve your personal problems. If you ignore developing yourself as a person while you develop yourself as an athlete, you are simply building castles in the sand. When the storms of life beat against you, everything you've worked for can easily come tumbling down. And the greater your sporting fame, the louder will be the sound of the crash.

> Is your athletic experience like a sandcastle? Have you experienced the storms of life beating against your castle?

Why isn't winning enough? It's quite simple, really. God designed human beings to need him in their lives. Only his agape love in their heart will give them a sense of self-worth that won't go away. Without God in their lives, human beings are trapped into using their talent to find some reason to like themselves. They expect their accomplishments to make them feel good about themselves. But God has reserved this role for himself alone. As a result, human beings always end up disappointed by the results of every achievement. And because they often overlook the needs of others in their pursuit of success, they can easily also end up alone.

Athletes are no exception. Most go through life expecting to feel good about themselves as long as they are winning and the crowd is shouting its approval. They are soon disappointed, however. It doesn't take long to discover that the thrill of victory is so very short-lived. But because they have learned to think that achievement is the only way to be fulfilled, top athletes stay on the treadmill. They tell themselves that the fame, fortune, and easy short-term relationships that come with being a sports star is the best possible life there is. So they keep straining for the next accomplishment, hoping that it will make them really feel content and satisfied. But deep down, they remain insecure. They don't know how long the good times will last or what lasting value they will have when the good times are past. And because their single-mindedness has often hurt those around them, they can only wonder who will want to be with them when their sporting career is over. They may be winners in sport, but they're surely losing out on life.

> Where would you be if you had to give up your sport today?

Christian athletes, however, take a different approach. They look at the vast expanse of the universe, governed by discernible laws not chaos, and they see an architect – God. They look at their own bodies, how ingeniously the human anatomy has been designed, and they see the handiwork of their Maker, not an accident of an impersonal process. They look into their heart, feel a longing for love, and they see the fingerprints of a God who so wants to have a relationship with them, that he has created them to desire what he alone can give. Stepping off the treadmill, they decide to stop living for sport alone and begin to learn about the source of life.

They look into the Bible, recognize that what God has said about human nature is true, and they admit that it's true about them, too. They acknowledge that, despite all their best accomplishments, they can't find fulfillment on their own. They realize that despite all their best intentions, their pursuit of self-worth often causes them to hurt others in the process. They look into the Bible, recognize that Jesus is trustworthy, and they lean on God's promises for forgiveness and new life through Christ.

> Do you know any athletes that have found real joy in life and have become the best in their sports?

In Jesus, Christian athletes find the release, relationships and reputation that alone satisfy their deepest longings. As a result, their faith in Christ acts as a rock-solid fireplace, so strong that their intense competitive desire can safely burn, warming their heart without destroying their life. Because of Jesus, they don't have to misuse sport by trying to earn self-love through it. Because of Jesus, they know they have a worth that won't go away. Not expecting sport to prove their importance or solve their problems, Christian athletes can once again enjoy the pure pleasure of physical release that comes through pushing their body to the limit. Not expecting sport to prove their importance or solve their problems, Christian athletes can once again begin to enjoy meaningful relationships with other sportspeople, even competitors. Not expecting sport to prove their importance or solve their problems, Christian athletes can enjoy a reputation for being real athletes who are also REAL. Not expecting sport to prove their importance or solve their problems, Christian athletes can once again really enjoy their sporting journey. Because Jesus has opened the door for them to have real joy in life, they can recover real joy in sport.

> Do you know this type of freedom that only comes through knowing Jesus?

To be the best, the very best God's agape love can make

you. To stand on the solid rock of Jesus Christ with choirs of heavenly angels on their feet for you. To be shown all the lives that have been touched by *your* love. To feel the Father's arms around *your* neck. To hear God Almighty say in *your* ear: "Well done, my good and faithful child. Share my joy, real joy, forever." Through trusting in God's promises, everyone can live that dream! Because Jesus is the best way.

Notes

1 • See William Nack and Lester Munson, "Special Report: Sports' Dirty Secret," *Sports Illustrated*, July 31, 1995, pp. 62–74.

2 • *The New Yorker*, June 1, 1987, p. 30, a cartoon by Edward Koren.

3 • Robert L. Short, *The Gospel According to Peanuts* (Atlanta: John Knox Press, 1965), pp. 35–6.

4 • Adapted from Margery Williams, *The Velveteen Rabbit* (New York: Simon & Schuster, 1983), pp. [3]–[6].

5 • Robert L. Short, *The Gospel According to Peanuts* (Atlanta: John Knox Press, 1965), p. 35.

6 • "Vikings Beat 49ers Despite a Long Run to the Wrong Goal," *New York Times*, October 26, 1964.

7 • Garrison Keillor, *Lake Wobegon Days* (New York: Viking, 1985), p. 135.

8 • Augustine, *Confessions* (Cambridge: The Loeb Classical Library, 1912), 2.4, 6; author's translation.

9 • "Such teachings come through hypocritical liars, whose consciences have been seared as with a hot iron" (1 Timothy 4:2).

10 • Kurt Cobain, "Dumb," as printed on the insert from *In Utero* by Nirvana, Geffen Records, Inc., 1993.

11 • Ann Landers, "Heaven and Hell – the Real Difference," as quoted in Jack Canfield and Mark Victor Hansen, eds., *A 2ⁿᵈ Helping of Chicken Soup for the Soul* (Deerfield Beach, Florida: Health Communications, Inc., 1995), p. 55.

12 • "In the congregation I will praise you. You who fear the LORD, praise him! For he has not despised or disdained the suffering of the afflicted one; he has not hidden his face from him but has listened to his cry for help" (Psalm 22:22b–23a, 24).

13 • "God made him who had no sin to be sin for us" (2 Corinthians 5:21a).

14 • Author's translation

15 • The Bible clearly describes this mindset and God's attitude to it in Romans 8:7-8: "The sinful mind is hostile to God. It does not submit to God's law, nor can it do so. Those controlled by the sinful nature cannot please God."

16 • John Stott, *The Message of Romans: God's Good News for the World* (London: Inter-Varsity Press, 1994), p. 67.

17 • In John 16:7b-8, 13, Jesus said, "Unless I go away, the Counsellor will not come to you; but if I go, I will send him to you. When he comes, he will convict the world of guilt in regard to sin and righteousness and judgment. But when he, the Spirit of truth, comes, he will guide you into all truth."

18 • "[God] set his seal of ownership on us, and put his Spirit in our hearts as a deposit, guaranteeing what is to come." (2 Cor. 1:22); "And by [the Holy Spirit] we cry 'Abba, Father.' The Spirit himself testifies with our spirit that we are God's children" (Romans 8:15b-16).

19 • "Surely the arm of the LORD is not too short to save, nor his ear too dull to hear. But your iniquities have separated you from your God; your sins have hidden his face from you, so that he will not hear" (Isaiah 59:1-2).

20 • See Josh McDowell's development of C.S. Lewis' original insight in *More than a Carpenter* (Wheaton, Ill.; Tyndale House Publishers, 1977), pp. 26-35.

21 • Author's translation.

22 • Mrs. Don Lash, letter to the author, December 4, 1995.

23 • Arthur J. Daley, "Two World Marks Set as Best U.S. Olympic Track Team Emerges From Trials ," *New York Times*, July 13, 1936.

24 • "Sullivan Award to Lash," *The Amateur Athlete*, January 1939, p. 19.

25 • I would like to express my appreciation to the following people who were helpful in providing information for this reconstruction of the 1936 5,000 meter Olympic Trial: Mrs. Don Lash; Hal Bateman, Historian/Statistician, USA Track and Field; and Richard Hymans, ATFS. In addition to those already cited, other sources used include: *The Los Angeles Times*, July 13, 1936; Richard Hymans, *The United States Olympic Trials for Track and Field 1908-1992* (Indianapolis: USA Track & Field, 1996), pp. 100-101.

26 • "The Man Behind the NCC: Indiana's Don Lash," *Sharing the Victory Magazine*, The Fellowship of Christians Athletes, January 1994, p. 19.